Up The West Coast of Australia

Daniel Mackler
www.wildtruth.net
New York City, 2018

ISBN: 9781980590453

A memoir

Dedicated to the
kind people who
pick up hitchhikers

Some names and identifying
information have been changed
to protect people's privacy

Chapter 1

At seven a.m., with three hours of sleep under my lack of a belt, I found myself in the parking lot of yet another roadhouse, this one on the northern end of Perth, the capital of Western Australia. Sunrise was still fifteen minutes away. It was raining lightly, and I realized I had left my umbrella in the backseat of Eric's car.

I had woken up forty-five minutes earlier on Eric's couch, roused by Eric, who was heading off to work. He told me he could drop me off on the way at a spot from which I could catch myself a northbound lift with a truckie. En route, he'd given me a whirlwind tour of the city.

"Aah, Perth's a bloody hole, mate," he had commented. "'Specially now in June. Good on ya for gettin' the piss outta 'ere."

The parking lot was presently empty. There were a few cars at the petrol pumps, but they were commuters, heading south into Perth for a day's work: no good for me.

As I walked toward the roadhouse, I wondered if there was a pay phone inside. I wanted to call my parents to tell them I was okay, but more so, to find out how they were. They'd split up nine days earlier, back home. My dad had left my mom.

Chapter 2

I entered the roadhouse, which was a small, ugly Quonset hut. It tinkled like a garden of bells in the light rain. I closed the screen door behind me and blinked my eyes to acclimate to the harsh, fluorescent lighting. I looked around and saw no phone—and felt a bit relieved. A big part of the reason I was out here alone, off the grid and so far from home, was to be away from them.

The cashier, an attractive, freckled girl of about twenty-five, looked me over.

“Ya hitchin’ north, mate?” she asked pleasantly, though with a certain toughness.

I felt shy and nodded my head. I wiped the raindrops off my face.

She continued: “Nah, mate, unfortunately them truckies headed north don’t stop heah.”

My heart dropped. She went on.

“And besoids, they don’t usually leave Perth ’til late at noit anyway. So ya’re either twelve hours too late or twelve hours too early—take ya pick.”

“So what do you think I should do ’til then?”

She smiled demurely at the realization that I was foreign. A dab of saliva pooled on her lower lip. She spread it around with her tongue and it glistened under the lights.

“Walk, I s’pose,” she replied, gently now, pointing to the north. “You a Yank?”

Chapter 3

I trudged northward sloppily through the wet grass on the side of what Eric had told me was the Great Northern Highway. It curved smoothly for miles but lacked a shoulder. It had a stone curb instead, making it impossible for cars to pull over. Not that it even mattered. The northbound lanes were essentially empty, with just a few scant cars zooming by too fast for me to hail them down, their windshield wipers cranking away the drizzle.

It was my first time alone in three days, my first chance to think. A week and more than two thousand miles earlier, in Melbourne on the East Coast, I'd called home to tell my parents about my plan to hitchhike around Australia. I had just finished a semester as a biology exchange student at Melbourne University and was officially free. That was when I'd heard the news—and it had caught me by surprise.

My mother had wept on the other end of the line and told me that my father had moved out. They'd been married for twenty-four years—since 1969, a month before Woodstock.

I'd been staying at the home of a university friend, and she and her mother had heard me crying from the other room.

I'd also cried in front of two of the rides who had picked me up since Melbourne. One was Eric's dad.

Chapter 4

An hour later, my shirt and hair wet, I arrived at a filling station. It was larger than the first, with a wide, paved area for even the biggest trucks to pull in and take their naps. They were called road trains here, because they pulled two or three hitches. There were presently three parked off in the far corner, curtains drawn and drivers presumably asleep: off-limits to me.

There was, however, a truckie filling up at the pumps, a little wiry guy with a thick handlebar mustache. I walked over to him, weighing "hi," which would identify me as foreign, against "g'day mate."

"Hi," I said.

"G'day, mate," he replied cheerfully, sliding the fuel nozzle into his second tank and locking it in place.

"By any chance you headed up north?"

"Sorry, mate." He leaned forward to read the diesel gauge and lovingly patted his truck's flank. "Just finished a run meself."

And it was true: his truck had no trailers attached.

But he still had information, so I asked him, more naturally now that he was no longer a potential ride, what I needed to know: how to get myself to a place from which to thumb it to the tropics. This road was awful and clearly went on forever.

"Well, mate," he said wheezily, "what ya're looking for is the North West Coastal 'ighway. An' she's, well"—with this he closed his eyes and seemed to be counting—"um, well"—I could see his eyes moving underneath his eyelids —"'bout anothuh, um, thirty k's up. Yeah, an' once ya hit the mouth of the ol' North West Coastal she's apples from there. Goes all up the coast, she does, faah's ya bloody-well want—straight to Broome."

"Thirty k's?"

Thirty kilometers was just over eighteen-and-a-half miles. It would take all day.

"Yeah, mate, thirty k's. Well, good luck to ya."

I thanked him and left to hunt around the roadhouse.

Chapter 5

I tried the car drivers at the pumps. They stood by their vehicles, miserably fueling up in the rain.

"Sorry, mate," replied the first, "headin' to work in Perth."

"Same 'ere," replied the second.

"Same," said a third.

And it was the same with the others.

I left them and went into the roadhouse station, where I bought some milk and used the bathroom in preparation for my trek.

On my way back to the highway, I sang "The Wayfaring Stranger" to myself, lullaby style. Halfway through the chorus, right where it goes up high, I noticed, out of the corner of my eye, the friendly little truckie waving to me from aside his cab—calling me over.

I strode up to him as I clasped by backpack to my body. I figured he had an idea for me, or maybe a question about America. Such things were not to be unexpected.

“Aay, so how ya goin’, mate?” he started, quite casually, screwing the cap on his second fuel tank and wiping his hands clean on a dirty rag.

“Hi!” I said. “What’s up?”

He wiped the back of his hand across his wet hair to push it off his forehead. “So listen, ya say ya’re headed up to the North West Coastal?”

“Yeah,” I replied, confused, considering he had been the one to have just given me that information.

He stuffed the dirty rag into his pocket, then looked me in the eye.

“Listen, mate, Oi can drive ya the thirty k’s. It’s really no worry.”

Chapter 6

Late morning found the two of us inching up the edge of the continent, 250 kilometers north of Perth: me, bouncing happily up and down in his padded passenger seat, him, merrily steering away. My backpack was stowed behind me in his little bed, which was half-hidden by two charming, decorated curtains that didn't match. A series of posters of naked ladies holding Australian beer bottles adorned the bedroom's back wall and a tattered replica of a Confederate American flag hung from the ceiling, fixed in place with rusty thumbtacks.

The short end of it was that the truckie, Caspar, had not in fact just finished a truck run. That was only his bluff to buy himself the time to feel out my demeanor and decide if I would make a worthwhile traveling companion. He was actually heading two thousand kilometers up the coast—over twelve hundred miles—to a town called Onslow, where he had to deliver seventy tons of cement powder, and then on to another town called Karratha. He showed me their locations on his map because I didn't have one of my own.

Five kilometers short of the North West Coastal Highway—at a point in which I still hadn't realized he was considering my fate—

he had pulled into a trailer compound, and in the middle of our blossoming conversation about our respective lives, told me he had to hook up some trailers to the cab and that I could wait in the truck if I wanted.

Still not suspecting, I'd figured he was trailering up to make a southbound run, so I used the time to update my journal, all about how I got to Perth with Eric's dad, Arnold. Arnold owned and operated a hauling company. He'd picked me up in the rain outside of Kalgoorlie three evenings earlier, where I'd been dropped off by a born-again Christian couple who had tried for two-and-a-half hours to convert me. I had made the mistake of telling them about my parents' separation, and they had used that for leverage to get me to come to Jesus. I had felt violated.

Later that night Arnold had let me sleep on the floor of his motel room. I'd repaid him the next morning by unloading about five thousand pounds of heavy wooden furniture at the house of his customer, a biker couple who thought I was his son because I did kind of resemble him and had said nothing more than "g'day." That was in Southern Cross. Later that day, Arnold had insisted I stay at the place of his son—"a young an' penniless bloke, jus' loik you, Dan."

Caspar had returned as I was finishing up a description, primitive drawing included, of Eric's gravity bong, which he kept under the kitchen sink in his apartment and didn't bring out until his father, who dropped me off there, had left. I wanted to build one when I got back to Swarthmore College in Philadelphia, where I would be entering my senior year in September.

"Mate," Caspar had said, "ya up for an offer?"

And aside from one small problem, the rest had been history.

Chapter 7

The problem was that Caspar had misunderstood my name back in the roadhouse of our meeting. He thought it was David, not Daniel, and I, figuring we'd only know each other for the next thirty k's of our lives, had decided to let it slide.

"David," Caspar had said (pronouncing it "Dive-id"), "Oi meself emigrated to 'Stralia from Edinburra—ya know, Scotland—as a little fella, a turd no biggah than ya bloody knee—but now Oi'm an Aussie through an' through."

Then: "David, East Coast truckin's a shit house rat race! Let me tell ya, mate…"

And: "Oi done it 'til Oi was twenty-noin, David."

Then pensively: "An' how old *are* ya, David? Ya look 'bout eighteen to me, *nah*, sixteen."

And explosively: "Twenty-one! Oi wouldn'ta believed it!"

And a few moments later (about halfway to the thirty k mark): "Not to be a sticky beak, David, but where are ya folks from, back before America?"

Then with surprise, after I told him about my father's side: "*Jews* ya say, David, well, then again Oi s'pose David's a Jewish name from the Bible an' all. David an' bloody Goliath. Now that Goliath was one big, bloody bahstahd, nah, but Oi'da run his arse down with this ol' road train!"

And then, somewhat calmer, with a shy and broken smile: "Oi me*self* got nothin' against Jews, David. They're good people, well, at least the ones down in Perth. They go to a temple."

And a bit later, as we neared the trailer compound, after a long diatribe about the Aborigines up north and how I had to watch out for them: "So David, whatta ya folks think about ya being all alone out heah in Westehn 'Stralia in the crazy yeah of 1993, ya know, mate, ya bein' not white, of a different race an' all?"

And once, by the time we'd started to get chummy, he even called me Davo.

"So tell me Davo, tell me about them little deer they got over there in that Florida, the ones that'll come right over an' 'op in ya lap if ya let 'em? Oi saw 'em on the telly last week!"

But this was all before I'd known I had a real ride with him. It was now too late to correct. And now that we were committed to each other for a two-day lift, David became my name.

Chapter 8

Three hundred kilometers north of Perth we outdistanced the rain. As the cloudy skies made way for the blue, the lush green of the southern landscape faded to a brittle yellow. No longer could we see the massive, rain-fed trees that had thrived around Perth, and the only trees left were remnants, shrunken in both size and density. The weather was becoming progressively hotter too, and we had to roll down the windows to keep ourselves cool. There was no air conditioning.

Scores of roadkill kangaroos lined the highway, in various states of decomposition. Some were quite large. There was not a single live one anywhere.

“Roos herd up during the day, Davo,” Caspar informed me. “They ’oid up in the ’ills to get out of the sunloit an’ only come down to the ’ighway at noit to feed. Ya’ll see ’em then. Fair dinkum, Davo, they’ll be bloody *every*wheah—an’ we’ll probably ’it a couple. That’s why Oi got such a big-arsed bull-bar on the front o’ me truck.”

As we passed a town called Dongara, Caspar was in the mood for music and handed me his box of cassette tapes so I could choose. That morning we’d already heard the best of Kevin Bloody

Wilson, including "Do you fuck on first dates?" and "Hey Santa Claus ya cunt."

In the mood for something different, I chose Midnight Oil—*Diesel and Dust*. I handed it over to Caspar, who fed it into the machine. The roaring bassline filled the bouncing cab. On "Beds Are Burning" we both sang along with the chorus, loudly, though I had trouble imagining Caspar agreeing with its support for the Aboriginal land rights movement:

> *The time has come, to say fair's fair,*
> *to pay the rent, to pay our share.*
> *The time has come, a fact's a fact,*
> *it belongs to them, let's give it back.*

"Caspar," I asked at the end of the song, "what's it really like up in the north with the Aborigines?"

"David," he replied, turning down the volume, "that's a very good question. *Very* good. Oi'd 'ave to say that at its *most* basic there's two toips of Abos: good ones an' bad ones. Most of the full-bloods are good people—ya *gotta* give 'em that. They keep to themselves on their settlements an' don't cause us whitefolks much trouble. An' with us truckies, them full-bloods 'ave learned to respect us, they 'ave, 'cause it's us that hauls in all their food an' grog. No truckies means no food an' no piss—and they bloody well know it. So they treat us good—respectful. Most Abos, Davo, are really nice people—an' up here we call 'em blackfellas. It's when ya get into the bigger towns that they start becomin' a problem and people take to calling 'em coons an' boongs."

"Boongs?" I asked. "What's that mean?"

Caspar smiled.

"It's the sound a niggah makes when 'e bounces off the bull-bar of ya truck."

He laughed and honked the horn twice.

"But seriously, mate, them are niggahs that nevah worked a *day* in their loif an' got *no* respect for the law. Mostly they don't trouble us whitefolks an' just sniff petrol an' tear each othah apart. Them're the ones ya gotta stay away from, mate. Ya *he*ah?"

"Yes," I said, nodding politely. Pretty much everyone I'd met on my travels had told me the same thing, including several of Eric's friends the night before. I, meanwhile, had been doing my own study of Australia's first people, the inventors of the boomerang and the woomera and the didgeridoo. There were presently about three hundred thousand of them around the country, probably less than half that from 1770, when the first white Europeans landed. They still spoke upwards of 145 languages, down from around seven hundred pre-colonization. And although they had been in Australia for fifty or sixty thousand years (and some say longer), they didn't comprise even 2% of Australia's population of seventeen million.

I wondered if I would meet any on this journey.

Chapter 9

Caspar went on to tell me that while he himself had never had a bad run-in with an Aborigine, he considered them a threat nonetheless. As such, he armed himself with a gun.

“A gun?” I asked, not unaware of Australia’s strict gun control laws, especially within vehicles.

“Yeah, mate, Oi got me own.”

He sat up straighter in his truck seat, proud. He had a wild glint in his eye.

I asked him if he’d show it to me.

“David, it would be *my* pleasure.”

Reaching with his free hand under a pile of pornos, which were under a pile of clothes under his bed’s mattress, he extracted the gun and passed it to me. It was a strange-looking contraption that came in two parts. Fitting them together, I realized what I had created—a single-shot, .22-caliber rifle. It looked like the kind of thing that would have been sold at a yard sale for ten or fifteen bucks when I was growing up.

"Mate, meet me daughter Alice. Alice, this is David. Yessir, David, took me six months o' networkin' to get hold of that little feminine piece of machinery there. Picked her up in Adelaide—had to shell out some 'aahd cash. Alice is a hot bird, mate, illegal as she comes!"

He reached over and caressed her trigger guard.

He then showed me his stash of bullets, which were hidden in a secret cupboard molded professionally into the ceiling. He also stored a canister of diet pills there, which he handed to me as well.

"Oi use 'em to keep meself awake on the longer runs. But they're nothin' compared to what the truckies take in the rat race out east. Bloody 'ell, them poor blokes are on everythin' from speed to coke to even *'aah*dah stuff." He shook his head. "It's a fuckin' dis*aaahs*ter!"

As he spoke, the North West Coastal Highway, which had returned inland, reached the dusty turnoff to Monkey Mia—the famed and unique spot where wild dolphins swim up to the shore and mingle with the human travelers who've carted themselves there for the experience. I had learned of its existence on a pub night in Melbourne a month or so earlier from my buddy Wombat—whom I'd met while hitchhiking down from Canberra a few months earlier. His real name was Warren, but everyone called him Wombat because of his resemblance to the squat, hairy marsupial.

"Go there if ya can," he had advised me. "Ya won't regret it. Plus it's free."

Alas, as Caspar and I roared past the turnoff at 80 k's an hour, who a month earlier could have known that I'd have found myself a ride up with promised sights set over a thousand kilometers beyond?

Chapter 10

With the coming of early evening, the sun stole behind the hills, the darkness rose, and nighttime enveloped us. At suppertime we stopped in a place called Carnarvon, where Caspar invited me to join him in a roadhouse restaurant. Having packed enough muesli, carrots, and peanut butter to last a few more days and wanting to stretch my budget, I fidgeted in the truck seat and finally told him I wasn't hungry.

"Absolutely bloody well not," he replied, hopping to the ground below. "No mate of mine stops in C'*naaaaah*vin an' eats birdfood. Don't think Oi wasn't watchin' ya nibble that granola crap there, Davo. It's not even cooked! Hell, my dog wouldn't even eat that. Nah, us truckies get discounts at these roadhouses an' Oi'll shout ya a steak an' chips, mate, yes Oi will, because that's just what *you* need right now. Now get ya arse down here!"

So I did.

The restaurant was a huge, single-level building with walls done up in wood paneling and an open, low-ceilinged dining area as expansive as an indoor market. It had a pleasant down-home atmosphere, despite the fact that its interior was segregated—by profession: simply, truckie or not. If you were a truckie, you got the back half of the restaurant, the better half, with the squishier cushions on your seats, the shapelier, happier waitresses at your service, and the wider, more decorated tables for your meal—not to mention one whole wall devoted to Polaroid photographs of the truckies themselves, each standing next to his own truck.

"There's me, Davo," said Caspar, pointing out his portrait, which looked more or less indistinguishable from the scores of others. Caspar, standing next to his orange monster truck, was tiny and faceless.

Caspar then walked me along the sacred wall and pointed out the best of his truckie mates, as well as the respective qualities of each of their trucks—engine sizes, fuel tank capacities, crash histories, and so on.

"There's L'il Jeffrey, Davo, an' Caspar Two—*only* two bloody Caspars in W.A. an' we're best mates!—an' Roland, an' Greg'ry. Ol' Greg'ry's a nut, mate, a l'il off—a few kangaroos loose in the top paddock, ya read?" Shooting his eyes around warily, he pulled me close and lowered his voice to a whisper. "Greg'ry's got a gun too, an' sometimes bloody shoots it out 'is window when ya pass 'im, just for the fuck of it. And 'e goes 'itting roos for the laugh, 'll bloody *chase* 'em into the other lane an' run 'em down if 'is blood's good an' 'ot for it! One crazy bloke *'e* is! Bloody *Greg*'ry! Crashed twice in nine yeahs, mate, goddamn awful! Lucky *Oi* picked ya up!"

Caspar then took me to an already crowded table, sat me down, and proceeded to order us steaks from the smiling waitress, a pretty young girl of about my age who seemed to have a special liking for him. When she turned to leave she wiggled a hip most flirtatiously in his face.

"Mate," whispered Caspar as she headed for the kitchen, "if Oi wasn't already married ya can bet ya bloody arse where Oi'd be spendin' *me* nights. Oi used to 'ave a whole string of ladyfriends up heah, just like her, ten or eleven of 'em. They couldn't get enough of me. But now that Oi'm hitched to the ol' handbrake Oi keep me paws clean. Lookin'—but no touchin'. That's what marriage is all about, Davo. Oi been married three months. Quite a bloody enterprise!"

Soon she delivered enormous steaks to our plates, and I dug in. Our table had a companionable male atmosphere and lay alongside tables and tables of other truckies taking their rest breaks from their respective northern and southern trips. Most of the guys were older, more weatherworn, and quite a bit more tattooed than

Caspar, who had only the letters L-O-V-E marked in blue across the fingers of his left hand. Some were completely decked out in ink, with everything from full-sized road trains crawling up their arms to naked women fighting jello battles amidst their chest hairs. As for me, quite un-tattooed and wearing a Navajo bandanna to hold in my rather long hair, I hardly looked the part of a truckie and found myself virtually ignored by the lot of them.

Chapter 11

The other side of the restaurant was for the Australian tourists—the side with stiffer seats, no camaraderie whatsoever, and a frowning squadron of older waitresses who took orders and served food with delayed, robotic precision and generally stood in bored impatience thinking only of cigarette breaks to come.

Looking over at a happily dining family, I decided that now was as good a time as any to try calling home. Taking a pause from my steak, I searched out a phone booth. After punching in the numbers and dropping in about two-thirds of my spare change, I found myself listening to a ringing phone—and suddenly had my mother on the line.

"Jesus Christ, are you alright?" she burst out.

"Yeah, Mom," I replied, scrunching my eyes shut as my psyche leapt continents. "I'm totally fine, a hundred percent safe. Everything's cool. I'm actually riding with a truckie right now—a trucker—up the coast of Western Australia."

"With a *truck*er?" she repeated. "Oh."

I cut to the chase: "So how's everything goin' at home? With, well, you know, you and Dad and all?"

I had been having a fantasy that she would say the separation had been a mistake—and that they were back together.

"Oh, it's okay," she sighed. "Dad's renting an apartment in Rochester now."

"But he hates Rochester!"

"Well, he's there now. He took a lot of his stuff over there with him, his suits and his CDs and his Maasai warrior poster."

The Maasai warrior: spear in hand, back tall and firm, face majestic, invariably unframed and taped to the wall. The Maasai warrior was one of my dad's more recent role models. My dad loved Africa but had never been.

My mom spoke on and on—about moving trucks, the weather, their half-empty bedroom, our family dog, telling the neighbors.

A pre-recorded woman's voice with an Australian accent interrupted and said that I had to put in more money or the call would be cut off. I put in the rest of what I had. I had two minutes left. But I could barely listen to my mother. It was overwhelming.

"–Mom, uh, I gotta go."

Silence on the other end.

Then a soft reply: "You gotta go?"

"I gotta go." I shifted from foot to foot in uncomfortable taps in the phone booth. "I'm, uh, right in the middle of dinner and the phone is going to cut off. I put in all my change."

"Dinner?" she asked. It was early morning in America. "Where?"

"Um, in Carnarvon—on the coast of the Indian Ocean. You can find it on the map up in my room. It's north of Perth, maybe nine hundred kilometers—about 550 miles—I'm sure it's there. Mom, listen, I *really* gotta go. I was just calling to check in and make sure everything's okay."

My tone was almost pleading. I felt myself sliding into something beyond my control. And I didn't want to cry here. I hadn't even told Caspar my parents had split up.

"You gotta go?" she asked.

"I gotta go."

"Bye, Daniel. I love you."

"I love you too."

I hung up, then stood in the phone booth for a long, quiet minute, feeling weird—and jarred and sad. A few tears pooled in my eyes, and I wiped them away.

Chapter 12

A couple hundred kilometers up the road I got sleepy. Having been up since six fifteen, I was dog tired and had an overfilled and slightly cramped stomach. Still wearing my boots, I wrapped myself in my sleeping bag.

"I'm gonna crash," I told Caspar, realizing from the look he gave me that I'd used an improper idiom for a truck. "Sleep," I clarified. I yawned and took out my contact lenses. "I'm gonna try and sleep."

And sleep I did. It came to me like nothing. It was nine thirty and pitch black overhead, aside from about ten million yellow, flickering stars. Only the healthy chugging of the engine and the rocking of the truck cab broke through the impressive night's silence.

At twelve thirty, I awoke to feel Caspar steering the road train into an obscure parking lot. I had been in the middle of a dream conversation with my father. We were in a sleazy tattoo parlor in Rochester and he was getting a tattoo of my mother's face on one thigh. I could see that he already had my face tattooed on the other.

"Do they mean something?" I asked.

“I don’t want to forget you,” he replied.

“Oi’se gonna have me a sleep,” said Caspar when he saw me stir. His first eighteen-hour driving shift had ended. He climbed up from his seat and into the hidden bed. Slipping under the fitted covers, he pulled the unmatched curtains closed to give himself some privacy. “Wake me up if Oi sleep past dawn.”

“Okay,” I said, yawning and letting myself doze back off despite the discomfort.

Truck seats, after all, were not designed to sleep long bodies like mine. I am six-foot-four—the same as my dad.

Chapter 13

At six the next morning, Caspar was up in a flash and welcomed me to the day by practically screaming in my ear.

"Good bloody mornin', Davo, an' a good bloody mornin' it is!"

He'd just taken one of his diet pills.

We both hopped out of the truck to breathe in the fresh morning air and pee—or "slash," as Caspar called it. It was still dark outside and now cold. Caspar rubbed his eyes and rinsed out his mouth with some water, then scampered back up into the cab to turn on the grumbly truck engine. Being five hours out of use, it was cold.

After brushing my teeth and putting in my lenses, I followed Caspar into the truck and fell promptly back asleep to the contented revving.

When I awoke, my sleeping bag crumpled in a ball beneath my boots and my back in a kink, I looked out the truck window and saw, to my amazement, that we had arrived in the Outback. It was dry and barren. The sun had long since risen over the land and swept away the morning chill. Opening my window, I breathed in the oven-dry heat. We were no longer living under the temperate effects of the southern wintertime.

Caspar began the day's talk by informing me that we'd hit four red kangaroos last night, one a muscular two-hundred-pound male.

"I didn't feel a thing," I said sleepily, pulling my sleeping bag up from the ground so I could curl back up into it.

"'Course ya didn't, mate," he laughed, his eyes glued to the road as we roared on past a dry riverbed that had gouged its way through the land of yellow dirt and gray, parched weeds. "This road train didn't feel a thing either. It sucks up anything that hops out in its bloody way an' spits it out the othah end."

As he spoke, my eyes alternated between the curving changes of the landscape and the shoulder of the road. The zoologist in me was on the alert for roadkill, out to meet the strange and interesting animals that only live here—the magpies and the bush hens, the walleroos and the possums. And as the hot wind drove away the last of the faint clouds, I found what I was looking for—a variety of dead creatures: eagles, lorikeets, galahs, kangaroos, and cows. Often, next to the dead and drying cows—or even embedded within them—lay the bumper of a car, or perhaps even its whole rusty, metal carcass, left for posterity.

Once I even caught sight of a dead echidna, the spiny anteater of Australia, the strange egg-laying monotreme whose closest relative is the platypus. It's a funny thing, a tough little ball of spines, not unlike a European hedgehog on the outside, but with a long, wiggly snout for sucking up ants and a completely different internal anatomy. As we passed it, my heart beat faster and I only wished for the chance to make a closer inspection—and even pluck a few spines for my natural history collection back home. But of course it was ludicrous to think of asking Caspar to pull over a loaded road train for such a seemingly trivial purpose. It had been hard enough to get my dad to pull our car over for such things when I was a kid.

"We almost hit a thousand pounds of cow last night, David," Caspar continued, obviously burning with desire to talk away the morning, "but Oi swerved off into the other lane enough to miss it."

With that, he jerked on the steering wheel to accentuate his point. The road train jumped into the empty oncoming lane of traffic, then onto the highway's far shoulder, and finally veered itself back into the proper lefthand lane.

“Yeah, mate, Oi almost killed us a cow, an’ take me word, *that* one woulda woke your arse up!”

Chapter 14

Early in the afternoon, some four or five hours of steady driving later, Caspar was to repeat this very maneuver—swerving the road train into the opposite lane—only this time it was no imaginary cow he would be swerving to miss. We were now in the outskirts of seaside Onslow, en route to the construction site that was his first destination. Rolling forward, we neared a ragged and intoxicated Aborigine weaving along the far side of the empty road. He was the first full-blood I'd seen in months and I studied him closely, reacquainting myself with the strange and exotic contours of his wide, dark face.

As we grew close, Caspar got the glint in his eyes and jerked on the steering wheel.

"If that boong comes any closer to the road, Oi'll make him into bloody meatpie."

At first I didn't realize he was kidding—and as the truck hopped across the lanes toward the man, my initial reaction was to grab the wheel and fight off Caspar. But amidst the tightening of my throat, he steered the road train safely back into our lane.

The intoxicated man, meanwhile, was oblivious. He was too far gone to have even the slightest idea that he'd nearly been grazed by eighty tons of cruising metal. As we flew past him, he weaved his way onward, directionlessly, up the gravel shoulder and into the desert.

"Niggah's high on petrol," said Caspar, shaking his head. "Oi shoulda put him outta his misery. Done this bloody country a service."

Chapter 15

Caspar and I spent the rest of the afternoon working to unload his seventy tons of cement—and work it was: a broiling, dusty, two-and-a-half hours of backbreaking labor which, under the ninety-five-degree sun, made moving furniture for Arnold seem like a tea party. Caspar's task was to drive a stout, yellow forklift between his truck and the fenced-in construction compound, and mine was to chain up and then unchain bag after one-ton bag of cement. I busted my guts and probably saved him a couple of hours.

The work bonded us and Caspar was now grateful to me, openly so. He treated me to a lunch of fish and chips for my effort—as well as a carton of orange juice to flush the cement dust in my throat through my system.

"Davo," he said, "ya were a bloody *maah*vel to behold—an' 'ere Oi thought ya was jus' a bookworm. Take another caahton of OJ. Go on, mate, it's on ol' Caspar McGibbons."

After Onslow, the two of us, sweaty and tired, roared the eighty kilometers back to the North West Coastal Highway. The wandering Aborigine was no longer in sight and it was now a desolate drive, without a single person or tree or animal. The only things that broke the monotony were enormous, gray termite mounds, known locally as "anthills." They studded the desert landscape as far into the distance as I could see. There were thousands of them, each shaped like its own miniature volcano, the tallest reaching ten or fifteen feet high. We'd learned about them back in my animal ecology class at Melbourne, the focus of our interest being that they functioned like giant, humidity-controlled, air conditioning systems for their hundreds of thousands of jointed residents, each of whom had its own specified duty—workers and soldiers and kings and queens. Hot air seeped into the bottom of the hill at its curving base and rose through the protected innards due to relative temperature, condensing along the way and leaving the nest below bathed in a cool, moist, livable temperature.

As we headed for Karratha, Caspar's final destination a few hundred kilometers to the north, the only event of any consequence came when I was randomly flipping through my address book. There I stumbled across the address of an Australian friend of mine from Melbourne, Nigel, who had a family home in Karratha. He'd known I was going hitchhiking and had given me his address in the unlikely event that I ever passed through his random, faraway village. He'd told me his parents had a couple of extra bedrooms, and that sounded lovely right about now.

Meanwhile, as fate would have it, Caspar told me that after Karratha he'd be turning around and making a run back down to Perth, at which point he'd be heading back north again, but this time past Karratha, all the way to a town called Port Hedland. The short end of it all: he offered to pick me up along the way, in Karratha, and take me to Port Hedland.

Ecstatic, I readily agreed—of course!

Chapter 16

An hour later, in front of the Karratha roadhouse, a lone building about ten k's out of town, I took Caspar's address and he took my friend's address and telephone number.

"So listen, mate," he said, shaking my hand tightly as we stood below his truck door. "Sometime tomorrow Oi'll be callin' ya at ya mate's house—this number 'ere—an' we'll finalize the plans. That good for ya, Davo?"

I nodded.

"Good, mate. *Good.*" Caspar looked down at his feet, then back up into my eyes. He paused for a moment. It seemed he had something else on his mind. "Could Oi ask ya to do me one last favor, eh, mate?"

"Sure," I said, curious. "*Any*thing!"

And it was true: for him I would do anything.

"In case Oi don't end up seein' ya again, uh, when ya get'chaself back to America, ya know, New York, the USA, could ya, *um,* write me a postcard from that, uh, Niagara Falls. Ya say ya live up there, *roit*, mate?"

"Yes I do," I said with determination, standing up proud and tall. "Sure do, I live less than two hours from Niagara Falls. I'll *to*tally send you a card. You can *count* on that."

I shook his hand to let him know I'd be good to my word.

"Well, David," he said, looking up at me sheepishly and twirling one side of his mustache between his thumb and forefinger, "the card wouldn't actually be for *me*, mate, it's, uh, for the wife. She fancies them cards an' things—*ya know*?—tapes 'em on the icebox, she does…"

I nodded.

"So ya'll do it?" he asked, staring back down at the gravel and then raising his gaze.

"Of course!"

"Good on ya, mate," he said, slapping me on the shoulder. "Good on ya."

And with that, he turned, climbed the metal ladder to his seat, and drove off south.

Chapter 17

The telephone rang.

I stared at it from the couch and resisted the urge to jump up and answer it. I'd been waiting for it to ring for hours. I was in Nigel's home and it was nine fifteen in the evening—just over twenty-four hours since I'd left Caspar.

Nigel's mother ambled into the living room from the kitchen, where she'd been cooking supper—fried fish. She picked up the receiver and cradled it between her ear and shoulder.

"Hello?"

I inhaled nervously. I had already warned her, as well as the rest of the family, that if a gruff-sounding Australian man named Caspar called asking for someone named David, it would be for me. It had been slightly awkward to admit to them that I'd let myself answer to David for nearly two thousand kilometers—and was planning to do so again.

"Why didn't ya tell 'im ya name was Daniel?" asked Nigel's father, a conservative, logical, mining engineer with bushy, blonde eyebrows and a faintly British accent. “Surely ’e woulda understood.”

I had shaken my head and tried to explain, but hadn’t been able to convey the diplomatic subtleties of the situation.

Now, blatantly eavesdropping, I stared at Nigel’s mother. She was grinning.

“*Nat*alie! So good to *he*ah from ya! No. *No*. *Won*derful. Good to hear it. Yes, yes, Nigel’s well. *Quite* well—got home four days ago, his semester went *maaah*velously. *Yes*. Yes. Engineering *an*’ maths. Yes. We’re *so* proud of ’im! *Yes*! Yes, adjusting quite nicely. *Heaps* of friends. Yes, *yes,* an’ one’s actually visitin’ us in Karratha *right* now. An American.” She glanced over at me and smiled. I nodded and did my best to smile back. “*Yes*! New York! No. *Haaahd*ly! Would ya believe ’e ’*itch*hoiked ’ere from *Mel*bin? *Yes!* Nigel thought it was a prank when ’e said ’e was calling from a roadhouse *in* Karratha. No! Arrived last night. No. *No*. Neighbahs at Uni. Yes. No. *No*. ’E’ll probably catch a lift out to the ’ighway with Thomas tomorrow mornin’ on his way to the mine. Yes. Mmm-*hmm*. Yes. *Won*derful. We took ’im on the scenic hike today. Yes. Fine, *fine*. A little hot, though—*of course*—but we brought water. Saw the Aboriginal rock carvings. Mmm-hmm.”

I stared down at my knees. No Caspar.

Chapter 18

The next morning, at the dark, ungodly hour of five thirty, I found myself back at the Karratha roadhouse, on the shoulder of the road and under the care of my thumb. There were millions of stars in the sky, and I picked out the Southern Cross—my favorite southern constellation. It helped me feel less depressed.

Caspar had failed to come through, and I had all morning of nearly trafficless silence to speculate on the reason.

Perhaps his diet pills had failed him and he'd crashed. Or perhaps he'd hit a cow. I hoped it was neither of these.

Or perhaps he'd called while we were out on the scenic hike. But then he would have left a message, wouldn't he?

I also considered the possibility that he'd had some change of plans and for whatever reason hadn't been able to call. Or maybe he had lost Nigel's number? Or had I written it wrong?

By eight o'clock the glaring sun had climbed over the hills. It was already up around seventy-five degrees and was clearly going to be a hot day. I gulped down some water. Nigel's mother had given me two two-liter containers.

A road train roared toward me, heading south. I moved away from the shoulder and waved to the driver.

He waved back and honked his horn and I shielded my eyes as he enveloped me in a vortex of wind and dust and sand grains.

I felt lonely. Caspar was not coming.

I missed him. It hurt.

Chapter 19

By ten thirty I'd managed to hitch fifteen kilometers north, to the northern end of Karratha. My ride was a sunburnt surfer on the dole who was on his way to the beach for the day.

"Ya were 'itch'oikin' from a crap spot, mate. More traffic where Oi'm takin' ya. Take me word. Ya coulda been stuck there all bloody day."

By eleven thirty I'd hitched another ten k's up the road, where I was picked up by a chubby, jolly auto repairman with a five o'clock shadow. His name was Murray. He was from a seaside town up the road a bit, called Wickham, and he made no attempt to contain his joy at having picked up a hitchhiker from New York.

"Bloody 'ell, mite, today's my lucky day!"

With no further ado he asked me if I had an hour to spare. Although I wanted to make distance, I didn't want to dampen his gleeful mood—and I was, admittedly, rather curious about what he had to offer. So I said yes.

Clapping his hands together, he laughed deeply, rubbed his belly, and exclaimed, "Fair dinkum! Now Oi can show ya Wickham!"

And so I saw Wickham, compliments of a Wickhamite. From the passenger seat I saw Wickham's golf course, elementary school, and high school, all of which proudly served Wickham's population of two thousand. I also saw the Wickham Hotel and learned that it had recently lost its liquor license.

"'Aaaahd to find a decent place to sink some piss with ya mites," Murray confided. "A shame, it is."

He then drove me up and down streets in a few residential neighborhoods and filled me in on the town gossip, of which he was keenly abreast. I learned who'd bought a boat, who was putting slate siding on their house, and who was slyly copying the idea. I also learned the cost of both new and old houses as well as the cost of a good plot of land overlooking the sea. It wasn't cheap.

"But worth every penny, mite! Don't let 'em fool ya. A quality community 'ere. Oi wouldn't trade me life in Wickham for anywhere—'specially not a city. Best place in Oz, faah's Oi can reckon."

He then asked me about New York—New York City, that is, that being his interest—not my little town up on Lake Ontario, that was actually closer to Ohio. He cringed at my description of the traffic and the noise and the throngs of people and the acid rain.

"No, mite, that is *not* for me. Not for me at *all*." He then looked down. "But Oi must admit, it's not all apples 'n' cream 'ere in Wickham. We got our share o' problems too, Danno."

He then drove me through the neighboring Aboriginal town, which had a population size similar to that of Wickham, but not even an incorporated name. It was a sad, rundown place, full of overweight, full-bellied Aboriginal women walking around barefoot or in flip-flops. I saw junked cars on people's lawns and several tiny kids left all alone. Some of them looked ill, and one was crying.

But I wondered if I was missing something—the family life, the life behind closed doors, the life off the road. I was hesitant to judge. After all, my family was a mess—but not all bad.

Murray shook his head.

"No, mite, it's sour heah. Oi wouldn't even know where to begin. If these people want a better loif they 'ave to adjust their ways—an' take proid in a new way of loif. But they don't. They don't want to evolve. Take the crime rate: nearly a 'undred times that of ours in Wickham. An' mostly the Abos do it to each othah."

"Hmm," I said.

"But enough of this—Oi just wanted ya to see it. Let me take ya home, mite. Oi want ya to meet me kids—twins—boy an' a girl—eleven. Oh, the little ankle biters aah gonna love you!"

Chapter 20

"I brought ya home a Yank!" Murray declared upon our arrival in his home, picking up a squirming, sandy-haired youngster under each of his doughy arms.

Then, turning to me: "Their fiihst *ev*ah…"

After a quick tour of the house and a peek at some family photo albums, we hopped back in the car so he could drive me to Roebourne—a better town, he said, for catching a northbound lift. Murray packed along the kids for the "cultural experience." Neither child, he told me, had ever traveled further than a hundred kilometers from Wickham.

"And bloody 'ell, to think they nevah even saw *rain* until they were three years old, what with the Great Drought of the eighties. Ya shoulda seen Johnno, mite, runnin' into the house cryin' an' screamin' fur 'is mum, 'is nappies 'angin' 'alf off 'is bum! Thought someone was sprayin' 'im with a *gaaah*den 'ose."

I avoided looking at poor Johnno as Murray spoke. Both my parents used to say embarrassing things about me in public when I was a kid, worse things than Murray was saying, and I'd hated it.

And they’d never listened to me when I told them not to do it.

Chapter 21

My pack over my shoulders, I ambled across Roebourne. In my hand I carried a satchel of sugary peach puffs and soft raisin cookies, compliments of Murray: "Baked by the wife!"

About a kilometer later, having passed entirely through the silent yellow-and-brown community without having been passed by a single car, I found myself a solitary spot on the edge of the void, a place where the highway bent at a ninety-degree angle. This all but forced the passing traffic to a halt—perfect for me. Now I could look them in the eyes—always an advantage when hitching.

Claiming the shoulder, I sat down on my backpack and waited for the cars to come. And come they did, one every twenty minutes or so. Mostly they were whitefolks. They passed me with their windows rolled up and their eyes averted, ignoring the pleas of my thumb. I tried sticking out my lower lip to further spark their interest or pity, but not a one put on its blinker, and if the drivers paid me any attention at all it was only to pass along a quick shake of the head.

At one point a small car full of serious-looking, long-haired Aboriginal men passed me, each a deep brown. Despite the fact that there was no room for me I stood up from my backpack and put out my thumb, as if to prove to them—and perhaps myself—that I lacked a racial preference when hitchhiking. It made no difference, though. Their icy eyes just skimmed across my face and they kept on going.

A southbound road train pulling three hitches of cattle passed me slowly, kicking up a wave of dust. The occupants shifted around and bellowed out unhappy moos as the driver navigated the tight turn. They smelled wretched in their hot, cramped cages. I figured they were off to a slaughterhouse in Perth.

An hour passed and I sipped water and ate a peach puff. It was excellent. I ate another.

Chapter 22

It was now mid-afternoon and must have been near ninety-five. I was completely exposed and had no sunscreen. I wrapped my spare t-shirt around my head as a turban and poured a little of my precious water into it. The turban smelled perfumey, as Nigel's mom had washed my clothes for me.

In the lulls in traffic, I scribbled feverishly in my journal. I had a lot to say, mostly about Caspar and how, even though he hadn't entirely come through, he had entirely changed my position on the face of the continent. There was no denying it; I was now in the north. I poured a bit more water into my turban and drank some too.

While writing I had a visitor. He was a tanned and rangy hitchhiker of about my age, carrying only a small cloth pack, a modest jug of water, and a fishing pole. As he strode past he acknowledged me with a dip of the head and a silent twitch of his dry lips. A few hundred feet up the road, he seated himself as second in line and took to staring at the pavement.

I scribbled a few more pages and found myself feeling bad for him. Second in line and hardly any traffic.

Then came the kicker: a third hitchhiker!

He was plump and about thirty-five and wore a wide-brimmed straw hat on his head to keep the sun off his face. He held a soft, sporty suitcase in one hand and a guitar case in the other.

Perking up, I invited him to sit down and play a song. I played guitar too, but had my guitar stored at Wombat's place in Melbourne. I'd been too scared to bring it on the road with me, especially because it had been raining heavily when I'd left Melbourne.

"Nah, mate," replied the hitchhiker. "The sun's 'aaahd on the guitaah. But if ya make it up to Broome maybe ya can hear me play then. 'Opefully Oi gotta gig in a blues club up theah."

With that, he tipped his hat and strode up the road to accept his miserable fate of third in line. For all I knew he'd be there until tomorrow.

Chapter 23

An hour later, my pen hot and my journal a protracted grammatical mistake, I managed to catch myself a lift. The guy that popped on his blinker to save me offered to take me to Port Hedland, the next sizable town to the north, and, incidentally, the very place to which Caspar was supposedly heading today.

Waving as I passed the other lonesome hitchers and reveling in the air conditioning, I rolled off with my new ride into the wild desert country. He wore the clothes of a businessman and told me he worked as a landscaper in connection with the main industry of the Australian northwest—mining. His job began when the mines pulled out of a tract of land, their work complete. He was paid to replenish the terrain with special fertilizers and replant a semblance of trees and other native vegetation across its surface, the idea being to recreate the original habitat.

“Does it work?” I asked, yawning from the day’s exhausting efforts and sinking pleasurably low into my seat.

“Nah, mate,” he stated dryly, “not really.”

“Hmm,” I said. My eyelids felt heavy. I let them close a little—such luxury.

"Nah, the damage of a bloody minin' operation's essentially irreparable to an 'abitat—what when ya consider they rip its guts roit out. Oi can give it a facelift at best. Yeah, 'bout three or four yeahs back there was talk of enactin' some new legisla-"

Chapter 24

"G'day, mate," said a gentle male voice.

Something nudged my arm.

"Welcome to 'Stralia, mate."

It nudged my arm again, this time more forcefully.

"G'day," I replied automatically, pulling my arm back.

I was presently in the middle of a conversation with my parents about my semester in Australia, though the real conversation was the unspoken one—about their separation. I felt from the look on my dad's face that he had a girlfriend.

"The ecology classes weren't bad," I said. "But I hated Philosophy of Science. The professor was awful. She was totally fake and boring and about as philosophical as a pinecone."

"So which end of town ya wanna get dropped off at, mate?" asked the voice, a bit rougher now.

I felt myself nudged a third and final time.

I opened my eyes and stretched my neck. It was cramped.

“Where are we?”

“Port Hedland, mate.” The man smiled faintly. “Bloke, ya sure can sleep. Ya’re like a dead roo. Ya just dropped off in the middle of a sentence there—an’ Oi was just gettin’ *staah*ted…”

“*Oooh*!” I sat up straight, cringing at the realization that I’d committed a cardinal hitchhiking sin. “God, I am *so* sorry! Mining! You were talking about mining.”

“Nah, mate, *nah*!” His smile burst wide and he poked me again in the arm, this time playfully. “Oi’m just takin’ the piss outta ya. That was two bloody hours ago! You didn’t even wake up when I stopped for petrol. So anyway, we’re in Port Hedland now. Welcome to the proud Capital of Nowhere.”

Chapter 25

I stood in front of a grocery store at the northern end of town. It was late in the afternoon and I knew that if I didn't get moving I might end up stranded there for the night. After filling up my water containers in the bathroom and buying a bag of apples and a liter of milk, I surveyed the area. On one side of the grocery lay a petrol station, presently empty. On the other side lay a bottle shop—an Australian liquor store—with a customer.

It was an old junker of a pickup truck, parked diagonally in the gravel—and packed with full-blooded Aborigines. About fifteen were squeezed into the large, fenced-in, back area, which seemed to have been erected to keep people from falling out. They were a rowdy, talkative bunch, hopping around practically on top of one another, and from their commotion it seemed they'd been drinking. I was tempted to walk over to them to get a closer look, but I didn't because it didn't seem they were good for hitchhiking and I didn't want to come across as voyeuristic.

Slurping down my milk, I walked over to the shoulder of the road instead and held out my thumb. An intermittent stream of northbound cars rolled past, throwing me the usual surprised glances of people who weren't expecting to see a hitchhiker on their side of the road—and only got used to the idea once they'd left me behind.

As always, I tried desperately to convince them of their grave mistake, but my efforts proved fruitless. Five cars passed. Then ten. Then fifteen. I hung my thumb low.

I wondered if my dad did have a girlfriend. It would actually explain a lot. I would have to suss it out when I got home. I didn't want to ask either him or my mom over the telephone. My dad would just deny it and resent me and my mom would do what she'd always done and make me into her confidant—which would make me resent her. Either way it was lose-lose. I gritted my teeth.

Chapter 26

As I descended further into thoughts of my parents, I heard a voice. It was a loud, female voice from over by the bottle shop. It was the voice of an Aboriginal woman—and I sensed she was calling out to me.

"Heyaa boy!" she yelled out deeply. "Boy! *Boooooy*! Boy! Heyaa boooooy!"

Not wanting to be too conspicuous, I snuck a quick side-glance over my shoulder and saw the voice's owner seated in the back of the pickup truck. She was staring in my direction.

She caught my glance.

"*Boooy*!" she cried out again from within the cage, doubling her volume and wildly swinging her bare arm above her head. "*Booooooooy*!"

Unsure of what else to do, I waved back. It was just a small wave, mostly from the wrist, but a wave nonetheless.

She noticed it immediately and used her arm to beckon me closer. Figuring I had nothing to lose, I threw my backpack over my shoulder and walked over. I took the time to study her pickup truck, and found myself questioning if it was actually a truck at all and not some sort of rusty, improvised dune buggy. For starters, it lacked many of the accessories I'd been trained to take for granted —like license plates, tail lights, parking lights, mirrors, and windshield wipers. On top of that, I could see that whoever had been responsible for repairs had sorely lacked spare parts. The fenders and side panels were crumbling and rotted and the bumpers had been replaced with wooden derricks, which were held in place with bungee cords and old cargo straps.

"Way ya goin' to, booy?" asked the woman when I came within a few yards. She stood up from her seated position amidst her companions. Like them, she was deep brown, but older, perhaps middle-aged, though I couldn't tell for sure. Her brow ridge protruded, her nostrils flared, and her lips were full and thick. She was also fat—probably technically obese. Her heavy, protruding belly and breasts stretched out the dirty midsection of her cotton, flower-patterned dress. Her legs, however, were thin.

"Pardon?" I replied, walking up to the edge of the truck for a closer look. The woman and I were now only separated by the three-foot-high chain link fence. I found my belly at the same level as her cracked, callused feet, upon which she wore an old pair of flip-flops—called "thongs" here—that had been repaired with duct tape.

"Way ya *goin'* to, boy?" she repeated, smiling now. It was a sincere smile, framed by her black, wavy hair, and it called the answer from my mouth.

"To Broome."

Broome, an old pearl-diving town, was an Indian Ocean resort hamlet a few hundred kilometers up the road—and the only place I knew in that direction.

"Oh, *Brrrroooome,*" she replied, nodding. Her face then grew quizzical, as if she were thinking something over. And she was: my fate.

"Get in," she stated firmly, motioning for me to hop over the fence. "We *all* goin' north too!"

I froze. I'd never been invited into anything by anyone Aboriginal before, let alone into a crowded cage with folks like this. Being so close, I could even smell them, and they smelled strongly of body odor and beer.

Yet the woman inviting me was kind. She emanated warmth.

I trusted her. And that made my decision for me.

Standing on my tiptoes, I handed her my backpack over the fence, then gripped the rusty metal rings and hoisted myself over.

Chapter 27

I leaned standing against the back fence wall, unsure of what to do next. The floor area was cramped with people. The larger folks were sprawled out everywhere and the younger ones sat scrunched in among them. I considered asking one of the youngsters to scoot over, but somehow it didn't seem tactful. So I waited, trying not to look awkward.

My friend got the hint. Having already seated herself along a side cage wall, she shook her hips roughly from side to side to free up a gap around her. Seeing my chance, I tiptoed toward it, careful not to step on anyone, and sat down—on a wide, wooden floorboard held down by ropes, one of the many planks that had been laid loosely across the decaying metal strip of original truck floor. In the slits between the planks I could see the gravel of the parking lot below. It did not look safe.

I clutched my backpack to me. My friend sensed my unease and draped her soft, warm arm over my neck and shoulder. For a moment I wanted to recoil from her, but then realized that I liked it in spite of myself. It was the touch of human contact: rare for me on the road.

Then a second Aboriginal woman, somewhat younger but with the same large body type, placed her hand on my bare thigh, just above my knee, and officially welcomed me to the truck.

"You *spunky*," she pronounced, slapping my leg somewhat roughly and then leaving her hand there. She receded her chin into the depths of her neck and flashed a coy, toothy smile. She then leaned toward me, motioned with her chin toward my friend, and stated in broken, beer-breathed English: "Don' bothah with her—she married."

I nodded politely but felt uncomfortable, even embarrassed. The arm on my neck suddenly felt very heavy and imposing, and I stiffened. The two women stared at me, seeming to gauge my reactions. I thought about getting out, but decided to stay and try to solve this. Wanting to interact with more than just two of them, I took a deep breath and sat up tall.

"I'm *Daniel*," I said, looking from face to face in the group and pointing to myself in case some of them didn't speak English. "My name's *Daniel*."

Chapter 28

Right away this changed the tone of the interaction. I met Delilah (my original friend, who took her hand off my neck upon introducing herself), Molly (her unmarried nemesis, who took hers off my leg), John and Amos (somebody's brothers, each around 250 or 300 pounds), and four or five other women by name and relation. A few of the other women just smiled at me or nodded.

The six men in the back compound (of whom John and Amos were only two) lay drunk across the planks amidst empty cans of Emu Export beer. They sported long, thick, black beards and wore tattered, grease-stained, collared shirts with many missing buttons that left their scarred bellies exposed. I wondered if they were brawling scars.

The ones who hadn't given me their names seemed hardly to notice me through their lolling, bloodshot eyes. For that matter, they seemed barely conscious of their own existences, let alone those of their drunken wives, upon whose laps their heads lay cradled. The wives, who were not so far gone, hugged and kissed and comforted them and slobbered wordless lullabies into their ears. One of the wives offered me an Emu, and had I not just finished my carton of milk I might have accepted. She laughed when I pantomimed the mixing of beer and milk in my belly and she pantomimed a look of subsequent nausea along with me. I liked her.

Three wary, little long-haired children with snot-lined faces watched me as well, their black eyes focused with childlike attention, as if they weren't sure what to expect. I smiled at them, but they soon lost interest and returned to peering out through the fence at the white miners who entered and left the grocery.

My eye also caught those of the oldest member of the group, a white-haired elderly woman. She sat the farthest from me, up against the far wall, her back stiff and upright. I had to sit up high on my plank to get a fair look at her. She couldn't have been much taller than five feet, and unlike the other adults was thin. But it was her face that struck me: a face that bordered on the edge of time itself, with dry, sunken, brown skin tightened over sharp, angular cheekbones.

She sat cross-legged on a plank, displaying a few remaining yellowed teeth as she cooed to an infant cradled in her lap. The baby was swaddled in some dirty, grayish cloth and was trying to squirm free. Its swollen face was a few shades lighter than that of everyone else, and I wondered if it had a white parent.

This idea set my thoughts in motion.

"I'm from New York," I told them slowly and deliberately, pointing to myself again. I wanted to make sure they knew I wasn't Australian, thus didn't hold any responsibility for the recent history of their land—the rapes, the massacres, the theft of almost their entire continent. "America—that's where I'm from. The U–S–A."

At this, they fell to chattering amongst themselves in what sounded like their native tongue sprinkled with English. Aside from some crookedly recognizable pronunciations of "Daniel" and "New York" and "America," I understood nothing. Their tones lilted musically, rising slowly then dropping precipitously, sometimes in staccato.

Suddenly the truck roared to life. To my pleasant surprise its engine sounded perfectly functional, humming as if it had been built yesterday.

But my pleasure wasn't long in lasting, for right then the final passenger of the bunch, a tall, gangly, puffy-faced Aboriginal kid of about seventeen years, ran across the gravel lot in jerking strides and climbed awkwardly over the cage wall to join us. Unlike the others, he was dressed in clean, new clothing. He wore a large, black Nike t-shirt, its chest area emblazoned with a looming, stone-cold image of Michael Jordan's face. The boy was drunk, and it took him more than a normal, dextrous teenage moment to right himself. His half-open, groggy eyes then began searching for a seat, at which point he saw me snuggled next to Delilah, just getting comfortable.

His eyes opened wide in alertness.

I smiled at him gently, hoping that he'd see me my good intentions and welcome me as the others had.

But he didn't. Instead, he narrowed his gaze and stared at me with unabashed displeasure. To make matters worse, the only empty spot was next to me. When this dawned on him, his face tightened further and he seemed prepared to remain standing.

Meanwhile, with all passengers present the truck jumped into gear and lumbered its way out through the gravel. This nearly tipped over the teenager and he had to hold on to the fence to keep his balance. Shaking his head angrily, he hopped roughly across a few people and plopped himself down beside me, such that our shoulders now brushed. He then cast his eyes downward.

Chapter 29

Out on the highway, we bounced up and down on our planks. Empty beer cans rattled around, the slumbering men grumbled on their wives' laps, and the children took their last forlorn looks at Port Hedland, which faded into the distance and blended with the bleak horizon. Late-afternoon yellow engulfed us and silence reined.

It was the teenager who broke it.

"Get out, white man," he half-muttered, half-whispered, turning his dark, peach-fuzzed face toward me. "Get *out* the truck. Ya not wanted here."

Unsure of how to reply, I pretended not to hear him. At this, he sat up and repeated himself, only louder now and with more authority, twitching his shoulder at the point where our arms met: "I say, get *out* the truck, white man!"

Compromising, I inched closer to Delilah. But that wasn't enough for him, such that our next round of communication came nonverbally—in the form of a violent poke at my ribs with his elbow, which I was lucky to deflect with a flick of my arm.

And that’s when it all began.

Chapter 30

You see, Delilah had been observing us, and she did not like what she saw. Rolling to her knees, she leaned across me and wagged her finger in his face.

"Have ya no *shame*, boy!" she shrieked at him in English. Her breath smelled of beer and tooth decay. "This boy here from New York, not Po' Hedland or Perth—*New York*!"

To her credit, it worked. Falling silent, he turned his face away from me and stared down toward Michael Jordan.

Delilah considered this a success. Sitting back down at my side, she emitted a loud grunt.

But her words had only a temporary effect. The boy, after stewing in silence for a couple of minutes, was soon back to muttering about me. Listening to him, I sat there quietly, anxious, unsure of what to do. But not Delilah. Rolling back to her knees, she leaned across me, shot out her hand, and grabbed his ear. The boy, jerking his head, managed to shake it loose, but this didn't stop her. Curling her chunky fingers into his face, she grabbed at his nose and lips. The boy realized his danger and buried his face between his knees in defense.

Delilah then proceeded to slap the top of his head, then push it downward hard, and finally smack his arms, her breasts swinging pendulously in her dress and bumping me in the face.

I felt torn. While I was glad she was sticking up for me, I didn't feel his actions warranted this assault.

Thankfully, though, she didn't seem to be hurting him. In his seated fetal position, he was too protected, so much so that she eventually gave up.

I sat up as calmly as I could and stared into the faces of the other people, in hopes that one of them had the wisdom to resolve the problem. But none did—not the wives, not Molly, not John or Amos, not the old grandmother. They all just stared back at me and refrained from intervening. It was as if it wasn't their battle.

And it was a battle.

Chapter 31

When the teenager emerged, it was obvious that Delilah's mission had failed. His face was twisted in fury. Jumping to his feet, he braced them on the plank and swung twice to punch me in the face. Both times I tucked in my head to avoid the blows and caught his fists on the top of the head, which hurt but probably hurt his hand worse. Infuriated, he grabbed my shirt at the neck with both hands and tried with all his might to heave me over the fence wall and onto the highway.

He only got me up about three inches, though, before my shirt ripped at the shoulder and I thumped back down to the plank.

At that moment the six drunken men awoke from their fog. Although I had written them off as incapacitated, they were not. Kicking beer cans out of the way, they plucked the teenager off me by his arms and legs and shirt and yanked him out into the middle of the cage. Holding him down on the floorboards, they proceeded to push him, poke him, slap his head and face, box his ears, and say harsh things to him in words I couldn't understand. Delilah, meanwhile, slapped him in the feet and legs with her hand—hard. Even Molly gave him a few kicks in the leg.

I crouched down to witness their version of justice. I'd read of their tribal spearings—an ancient form of corporal punishment in which elders calmly insert sharpened wooden or metal spearheads into the calf muscles of serious offenders. This seemed totally chaotic by comparison.

The boy fought back a little, but soon gave up. Rolling around helplessly in a sticky puddle of beer, he simply absorbed the torment coming at him from all sides.

I couldn't stand it. Welling up with agony, I sprang to my knees and covered his head and face with my hands, and his body with my own.

"Stop it!" I cried out. "Get off him! Leave him alone! Jesus Christ, *stop it*!"

Confused by my outburst, a few of the men paused to look up at me. The rest seemed oblivious and continued the abuse. One of them mistakenly smacked me in the ear with his open hand, knocking me over.

"Get off him!" I screamed out again, jumping back onto the boy and blocking their hands and arms with my elbows. "What the fuck? Leave him *alone*!"

At that point the rest noticed me and paused, releasing their grips on him and slumping back to their positions next to their wives.

Once the last of them had retreated—and Delilah too—the boy found himself free, with only me kneeling above him. I looked down at him for a moment, then crawled back to my spot. Dazed, he lay across a few planks like a wounded fawn and let out a pained sigh.

Chapter 32

The boy wiped his lips to see if they were bleeding, which they were. The lower one was split right down the middle. Aside from that, though, he didn't appear to be too hurt. I couldn't, however, say the same for his Michael Jordan shirt. It was rumpled pretty badly.

The boy took hold of it by the lower hem and pulled it down to cover his bulging belly button. As he smoothed out the soft, dirty, beer-soaked fabric, he noticed that it had a ragged tear on the side, probably from getting caught on a floorboard during the fray. He looked devastated. His face welled up with emotion and his body began jerking tensely, as if he might cry. Tightening his arms instead, he managed to gain some control over himself and then crawled dejectedly back to his seat next to me. Curling himself limply into another upright fetal position, he buried his face in his lap and began to finger his shirt miserably.

Watching him, I felt horrible and started to cry myself. My ear was ringing a little from the smack. Pulling my bandanna down from my forehead, I covered it over my face so no one could see me. Pulling my backpack to myself, I hid behind it again and tried to clean myself up. I blew my nose into an old napkin and inhaled a long, deep breath. The desert air smelled fresh, like wind and sun and dry Outback plants.

After a long minute or two, I peeked out from behind my pack and saw that the people were staring at me. Their dark eyes focused on my face. I felt shy—yet oddly confident, like I'd done something they found acceptable.

Delilah seemed to know how I was feeling. Placing a soft hand onto the back of my neck, she began to knead the knots in my muscles with her strong, springy fingers. This unexpected show of affection caught me off-guard, and triggered something deep within me. Bursting out with emotion, I began to weep, first quietly and then louder.

Chapter 33

The pickup truck lumbered onward and normal talk resumed. One of the women broke out with another case of Emu and passed out cans in all directions. One of the more forward children requested a can for himself but was denied and found his hand slapped with surprising deftness by the old grandmother. The cream-colored baby opened its gaping, toothless mouth at the sudden movement and began bawling. Delilah laughed.

I felt hungry and remembered the bag of apples I'd bought in Port Hedland. Digging it out out of my backpack, I kept one for myself and passed the rest along to Delilah. Choosing herself a good one, she continued the precedent by passing it on to Molly. Soon the whole family was busily engaged in a meal, chomping and chewing and swallowing and flinging out cores over the fence. Even the old grandmother took a little apple for herself, stabbing into it with her front tooth and prying fruit wedges into her mouth.

Delilah and Molly returned to vying for my affection, which again made me uncomfortable. As Molly leaned forward to rub my knee, her breast slid out of her low-cut dress. I pretended not to notice, yet I couldn't help but stare. It was large and round and its nipple gleamed purple in the late-day sun.

As I returned to gnawing my apple core, the children began to play. The baby cooed and giggled and the grandmother let it slurp apple juice off her fingers. The drunk men fell back into slumber on their wives' laps and the teenager looked contentedly out the fence wall at the passing desert scrub, some dried blood crusted on his lower lip. Delilah smiled sweetly at me and offered me a cigarette, which I smoked.

"Yah come Mababah, Danyo?" she asked.

"Mababah?" I replied cautiously. I assumed it was the name of their Aboriginal community off in the bush somewhere. "Is it safe for me to go to Mababah, Delilah?"

To this she smiled again, nodded, and tenderly stroked my arm.

"Yah come Mababah, Danyo. Yah come."

"I—I don't know," I stammered out.

But it seemed she had already made up her mind: I was going to Mababah.

Chapter 34

The sun began to set. The orange lights of dusk receded over the western hills and darkness swept across the land, a desert darkness that spread even faster than the wind. A half-hour later, some miles ahead, and at a totally nondescript spot, the truck applied its brakes and ground to a halt on the shoulder.

All at once, everybody began piling out of the cage and onto the road—even the drunk men. I had no idea what was happening, but I followed their lead, hopping over the fence and bouncing down to the road. I suspected the truck had broken down and that somehow they had silently communicated it to one another.

But no: slash break!

Most of them were drunk, after all. The men lined up in a row off to one side of the truck and began urinating, releasing quarts of metabolized beer into the thirsty, desert earth. I joined them, solemnly providing a token offering of metabolized milk. The women, meanwhile, chose the other side of the truck for their row—just out of our sight.

Then everybody climbed back in—except me. As I began to hoist myself up the fence wall, Delilah bounded up and put her hand on my shoulder, stopping me. Shocked, I thought I had unknowingly done something taboo and was being put out as a result. And when she ordered two of the children to fetch my backpack and hand it to me, I knew it was true.

But no.

"Danyo," she said, taking my arm and leading me away from the back caged area, "yah sit in de front with de men now."

Carrying my pack, I complied. Following her up front, I climbed in through the open passenger's door and took my place next to the driver, a tiny, elderly Aboriginal man who sat on the far right of the vehicle, as sober as I. He was smoking an unfiltered cigarette and he ignored me. Two middle-aged men, both enormous, salt-and-pepper-haired fellows, piled in after me. Delilah, standing aside the door, told them I was from New York and issued them all an order in English to leave me alone. She then said a few rather harsh-sounding words that I didn't understand. They did not reply.

She then ran off to the back and hopped her bulk in over the cage.

The driver, popping the clutch, soon had us off and rolling again and shifted from second into fourth—the only two gears of the truck. As we hit our cruising speed of about twenty-five miles an hour a gust of wind caught me in the face, dawning a strange realization in my mind: that the truck had no windshield. Only a spaceless gap separated us from the road, forcing me to squint to prevent dirt and desert bugs from getting into my contact lenses. I noticed the old driver was squinting as well. He also had both hands on the wheel. I appreciated that.

The two obese passengers, meanwhile, fell asleep. Both were so plastered on Emu—cans of which lay at our feet—that they didn't even notice me. The one nearest me was snoring, his head half-tilted backward, and the one in the window seat slept with his head banging rather sharply against the door frame. I wanted to adjust his head to a more comfortable position but was afraid that he might not respond well to being touched. So I let him be.

Occasional cars of rich, white tourists in modern VWs and Hondas passed us in the other direction, waving wildly to us and yelling out soundless hellos. Our driver, seeming used to this kind of attention, paid them no mind whatsoever. And despite the fact that it had long since been my habit to acknowledge any and every passing car, I paid them no mind either.

Chapter 35

We arrived at a dirt turnoff from the highway. The driver pulled the truck onto the shoulder and brought us to a halt in front of a green roadsign.

"Marble Bar, 156 kilometers," it read.

It had a long arrow pointing deep inland—into emptiness.

Marble Bar. I felt I'd heard of it before, somewhere, but couldn't place where.

Suddenly Delilah appeared at the window to check on me.

"Yah come Mababah?" she asked, pointing to the sign, at which point I realized where I'd heard it.

The driver killed the engine and the truck's lone headlight shut off. The sign went black and I realized how dark and impenetrable it had become outside—and cold. I was shivering. I still had on just a t-shirt—and a torn one at that.

Delilah looked me over.

"Stay in de truck," she said forcefully. Yet I also sensed gentleness in her voice, concern.

"Ah," I replied. "I don't know..."

Twisting my head around, I looked back at the others in the cage. I wondered how they felt about me coming along. It didn't feel right.

"I want to get out," I replied, rather loudly so the two men blocking me in would get the hint and let me out. "I need to get out."

But they didn't budge. They were both sound asleep.

"It's okay," said Delilah. "Stay in de truck. Yah come Mababah."

But it wasn't okay. I felt trapped. I had to get out. Grabbing my pack, I threw it out of the vehicle through the place where the windshield should have been—and then slid my body after it across the hood, boots first. I landed on the ground on the driver's side, opposite Delilah.

"Delilah," I stated as firmly as I could, standing up tall, "I'm not going to Marble Bar with you. I can't. I mean, I'm sorry, I really am, but I'm going on to Broome."

I nodded my head to get my point across. I felt strangely powerful—confident. My week on the road had improved my self-esteem.

"No," she replied bluntly, walking around the truck and joining me. "It cold an' dangerous on de highway. Yah *come* Mababah. Yah die out here!"

And as I stood there, my pack at my side, something in her words pierced my armor.

To be precise, it was the word "die."

I didn't know what exactly could kill me out here, but it didn't take much imagination to guess: there wasn't anything out here. No water, no people, no trees, no buildings, no signs of life, no sun, no traffic. Just wind and cold and dust and the faintest outlines of rolling hills in the distance—and some very bright sun to come tomorrow.

Chapter 36

I decided to obey her. Taking me by the hand, she led me like a child back to the caged area, where she seemed to feel I now belonged. I started to climb the fence, but as I was halfway up, my backpack dangling from my back, I was stopped—by, of all people, Molly.

"No!" she screamed, stepping across a horde of men and barring my entrance by shaking the rungs of the cage. "This *mah* truck, give to me by *mah* daddy, an' the white man stays out!"

She shot a ferocious look into my eyes, and added: "*Yah* not comin' in here, booy!"

But Delilah was right there.

"Have yah no shame, *girl*?"

And then Molly, hoarsely: "Yah *cunt*!"

With that Delilah started climbing the fence—at which point I, guided more by adrenaline than anything, backed away, and then turned and walked away. I had seen my parents fight enough times to have learned to stay out it. My interventions had only made it worse for everyone, myself included. And this wasn't even my family.

At twenty feet distance, I heard a man's shout break out, and then another's. I peeked back. Several men were standing to prevent Delilah from entering the cage. She was cursing at them and trying to hit them and Molly was still cursing at her.

"Cunt!"

"Cunt!"

It was at this point that something clicked in my head, something simple and quiet and strangely logical: *this is insane; this ride is over.*

Chapter 37

Their voices grew faint as I walked northward. The road ahead was silent and empty. A thousand flittering stars dotted the sky, and more were sure to come. I could hardly see the hills.

I lengthened my stride. It felt like a horrible way to end a ride, but I couldn't see any other options. I figured sooner or later, once the road got quiet—once they'd driven down the dirt turnoff—I could leave the highway and walk up into the hills with my tent, pitch it in the darkened, red earth of some hidden kangaroo valley miles from anywhere, and get myself some sleep.

But when I was a hundred feet up the road, my curiosity overcame me. Peeking back, I discovered that someone was following me, emerging from the darkness at a rapid pace. It was Delilah.

"Don't *goooooo*!" she cried out, half-running. "*Don't* gooooo! It the *desert* up dere. It *nighttime*. Yah *come* Mababah! *Don't gooooo*!"

I paused.

"Have *yah* water?" she yelled out, closer now.

"Yes," I called back. "Four liters. *Please,* Delilah, leave me alone. I *just* want to be left alone."

"No," she proclaimed, breathing heavily as she reached me. "Not enough water. It too dangerous—cold in de night, too hot in de day. If yah go, *I* go too."

"*No*!" I replied, an image of the two of us sharing my tent flashing before my mind's eye. "I mean, *no*, just no, I'm fine. I really am, Delilah. Please, *please* just go away and leave me be. I'll be okay."

"Have *yah* matches for fire?"

I nodded my head.

"An' a blanket?"

I nodded again but felt torn, unable to lay down the law and shake her off—especially without hurting her feelings. For all her antics, I still felt that she genuinely cared about me. In fact, I knew it.

As I wondered what to do, my answer came to me from the north —from way up the highway. It was rumbling toward us. As its sound grew louder and its small yellowish glow distinguished itself from the horizon, I realized the identity of my new option: a road train, barreling down to Port Hedland.

Hopping across the center line into the distant truck's lane, my pack still on my back, I held my hands up high over my head and started waving them.

Chapter 38

The road train approached with no sign of slowing down. As its headlights grew brighter and split into individual entities, I could picture the huge piece of machinery behind them—with its massive V-shaped bull-bar, its steaming chrome grill laced with a thousand dead butterflies and moths, and its little driver perched up in the window, deciding my fate.

Soon I heard its horn blaring. Ignoring it, I waved my arms faster and then heard what I was listening for: the harsh whooshing of escaping, compressed air—its air brakes. The behemoth was slowing down.

I glanced over at Delilah as the truck ground to a halt in front of my body. She had backed away, off the shoulder, into the dirt, and almost out of view. The expression on her face was a mix of shyness and fear.

The driver flicked his headlights off and on twice, which I took as my cue to approach the cab door. Staring up into his darkened window, which was rolled down a mere inch, I told the faceless gap that he'd better let me in. The window then rolled down an inch more and through the crack I saw a man. Well, actually, all I saw were the two frozen eyes of a pissed-off truckie.

Chapter 39

I changed my tone.

"Will you let me in? *Please*?"

The window rolled down a bit more and his angry voice shot out at me.

"What in the bloody *'ell* were ya standin' in the road like that for? Are ya fuckin' loony, mite*?* Oi thought ya were a goddamn roo!"

In response, I said what I had to say to get my point across: that I'd just been stranded there by a bunch of Aborigines. Thankfully Delilah was out of earshot.

"Look!" I said, pointing down the road. "*There's* their truck!"

He rolled down his window the rest of the way and popped out his large head, which was covered with a shocking amount of sweaty, red hair. I followed his gaze as he stared down the road.

"Jesus Christ, mite," he said. "Get in on the othah side. C'mon now, *fast*."

With my pack still on my back, I did as I was told. Climbing the ladder and slamming the cab door shut behind me, I dropped my pack at my feet. As I adjusted myself into the soft seat and put on my seatbelt, I took a moment to look him over in the dim light. He was about forty, an Irish-looking fellow with a trim, bristly, red beard and deep wrinkles on either side of his little, slightly upturned nose.

I peeked across him and out the window to get a last look at Delilah. She stood there half-shadowed, mute in her flower dress and duct-taped flip-flops, arms at her side. We made eye contact, yet neither of us acknowledged it.

The driver, still not knowing she was even there, kicked the truck and all its hitches into gear. Delilah was ripped from my view in an instant.

"Ya were bloody lucky Oi didn't flatten your arse out," he said. "Oi'm pullin' four hitches—largest legal load in 'Stralia." He lit himself up a cigarette. "But can't quite say Oi blame ya, mite. Buncha low-class niggahs."

I suddenly felt as if I might vomit. I was leaving them. Leaving her. Leaving her world. I felt like a deserter. And, as crazy as it sounds, I missed them. Tears welled up in my eyes.

The truckie went on.

"Nah, but ya got some balls flaggin' me down loik that. That's a first toim for me, it is. Oi really thought ya were a fuckin' roo. Oi coulda killed ya easy."

I was changing skins. I had escaped. I was rejoining the race of her people's conquerors.

I turned my face away so he wouldn't see me cry.

Chapter 40

I woke up the next morning in my tent. The air around my face was freezing and my toes were numb. It was six a.m. I was in a cheap campground in Port Hedland, not far from where the truckie had dropped me off the night before. He had invited me to join him and his truckie mates for an evening at the pub and had even drawn me a walking map to get there. He'd wanted me to tell them the story of how we'd met so they wouldn't accuse him of lying. But I had been noncommittal. I'd needed to be alone. Plus I wanted to write in my journal, which I'd done—a thirteen-page entry scribbled by flashlight.

After greeting the morning air, I showered, shaved, put in my contacts, and broke camp. My first stop was the grocery, the same one from yesterday—with the bottle shop next door. I bought another carton of milk and drank it as I crossed the parking lot. It was now empty. I found where our tires had dug tracks through the gravel fourteen hours earlier—and I thought of Delilah. I felt sad and confused, yet at the same time strangely proud that I had been included, if only briefly, in their lives.

I reached the highway and my heart sank with a surprise: another hitchhiker was already there.

And the second surprise: he was none other than the plump blues guitarist from the day before. There he sat, two fingers of one hand dangling over the white line of the road in classic Aussie hitching style, a half-eaten Mars Bar in the other. A thin line of chocolate was painted in a neat arc across his lower lip. He looked pleasantly bored.

"G'day," I said as I walked past him, trying to feel out his demeanor to see if he wanted to talk. He was the closest thing I had to an ally. He might just understand what I had gone through.

"G'day, mate," he said, patting his fingers on his guitar case and then dangling them back out into the road.

A car was coming. He focused his attention on it and ignored me. I got the hint and meandered up the road. The car passed us both.

Chapter 41

The spot I chose was ugly and exposed and directly across the road from a power line. But this proved lucky. Ten minutes later company arrived: a large goshawk. She flew down and landed on the line. She rested perfectly still, eyes focused on the dry grass below. She was hunting. For half an hour she didn't flinch a feather on her creamy, mottled breast.

Then suddenly she swooped and bounced to the ground, wings jerking in fury. A miss! She then flew back to a new spot on the power line. Focused again. Froze. Waited.

I ate one of Murray's raisin cookies and watched her for another half-hour, during which time the morning traffic dwindled to a trickle. She dove twice more and finally caught a small lizard. Gripping it in her talons, she flew away. I ate another raisin cookie.

Another hour passed. Several fleets of mining trucks drove by, smothering me and the road with red dust. The sun rose high into the sky and burned my brain. The blues guitarist had still not gotten picked up. In fact, he hadn't moved an inch.

I cleaned my fingernails with the smaller blade on my Swiss Army knife. The blade grew hot in the sun. The dusty cement of the road grew hot too.

I thought of Delilah—and wondered how she felt about last night. I wasn't sure how I felt. I fingered the raised bruises on the top of my head. They hurt, but I found the feeling rather pleasurable.

A third hitchhiker appeared on the scene. He was a lanky man of about forty-five, with long, stringy, blond hair and a thin, gold ring in his nose. He carried a stained, external frame backpack like my hippie uncle Dewey used to have in the seventies, and he wore a threadbare t-shirt with the word "Esperanto" printed in fading, multicolored letters on the chest.

"Hi," I said, smiling as he passed, hoping he would stop to talk. My voice was dry from the dust. I coughed in spite of myself.

"*Saluton*," he replied mechanically, making momentary eye contact but giving off the vibe that he didn't want to interact. But I couldn't resist.

"Is that Esperanto?" I asked to his back, because he was already beyond me.

"Yes," he said, and kept walking.

He settled a couple hundred feet up the road and looked away from me. He pulled a basketball out of his backpack and started spinning it on his finger.

I wrote some more in my journal, but couldn't get into it. My thoughts kept being intruded upon by visions of the boy who had attacked me. I wondered how he was doing—if he was sore from the beating he'd gotten, or hung over, or depressed. Me, I felt despairing. Also, I felt trapped as second in line, hopeless that I would never get a ride.

I decided to try meditating. I had been practicing back in Melbourne. Wombat, who dabbled in Buddhism, had been teaching me various techniques. Closing my eyes, I pushed myself to let go of my worries and enter the other realm—and join with nature. I was not very good at it, but I forced myself to try harder, so much so that I barely even flinched when two cars passed.

Then I felt a tap on my shoulder.

I opened my eyes in a half-panic. I thought—I kid you not—that it was Delilah!

But it wasn't.

It was the Esperanto guy with the nose ring. His backpack was slung over one shoulder, the basketball was out of sight, and he had a water bottle in his hand. He pointed down the road with his finger and I saw that the blues guitarist was no longer there. Evidently he'd gotten picked up. I felt silly that I had to be told the obvious, but I also felt relieved—because I was now first in line.

"Thank you," I said.

"No worries, mate," he said, and set down his backpack and took a swig of water.

Chapter 42

I claimed the blues guitarist's spot—my old spot from yesterday. But there were now cars at the petrol pumps, so I decided to give them a try first. It gave me something to do. I didn't like sitting with my own thoughts. Not this morning.

"Sorry, mate, no room."

"Sorry, bloke."

"Nah, mate, headin' into town."

I returned to the road.

Another hour later, the temperature feeling like a hundred, I was back at the petrol station. The first person I approached was a grim-faced, middle-aged man in a green truck.

"So ya're goin' to Broome," he said.

"Yeah," I replied. "By any chance are you headed that way?"

He looked like a miner. His clothes were red with dust.

"Oi am," he replied. "An' if ya want Oi can take ya to a turnoff a hundred-and-ten k's up the road."

"The turnoff to Marble Bar?" I asked suspiciously.

"Nah, mate, it's about sixty k's past the turnoff to *Mah*bah Bah."

"The Marble Bar turnoff's only fifty k's up the road?"

The significance struck me: if true, it meant my whole ride with Delilah and company had been only thirty miles. Walkable—at least at night.

"Yeah, mate, fifty k's, an' Oi'll take ya more than twice as faah. That okay?"

"Yes!" I exclaimed. "For sure—I'll take it! I just gotta run back and grab my pack."

"No worries," he said. "Oi'll still be a few minutes."

After shaking his callused hand to cement the promise, I sprinted back to the road—and decided to tell the Esperanto guy of my good fortune.

But he was suspicious.

"Hmm, how long's the lift, mate?"

"A hundred and ten k's."

"Where's this bloke leavin' ya?"

"At some turnoff—I'm not exactly sure."

"They got water?"

"I don't know. Prob'ly do."

"Ya sure?" His eyes flashed purple and his tone bordered on the aggressive.

"Well, I'm not positive…"

He shook his head definitively.

"Don't take the lift, mate."

I felt a twinge of fear.

"Why not?"

"D'ya wanna get yaself stranded in the desert?"

"Well, not really. I mean, I dunno."

"So like Oi said then, mate, don't take the lift. Ya could die of thirst. Even Abos die out theah. It's 'ot as piss—'ottest part of the

’ole bloody country! Reaches forty-fuckin’-five! Nevah take a lift unless they promise to drop ya off at a roadhouse.”

I looked down at my boots. Forty-five degrees Celsius was 113 Fahrenheit. He had a point.

I thanked him and walked glumly back to the petrol station.

“Um, I can’t take the lift,” I told the driver.

He lowered his sunglasses and peered out at me with surprise.

“Why?” he asked. He sounded almost hurt.

“I-” I nibbled my lip. I felt silly for my naivete. “I, *uh*, just don’t think it would be all that safe for me to get, uh, dropped at a desert turnoff. I mean, I don’t have that much water and–”

“*–aah*, bloody oath, mate,” he interrupted, slapping me on the shoulder, “if that’s all that’s worryin’ ya Oi can drive ya an extra thirty k’s an’ drop ya off at a nice roadhouse.”

“You can?”

“Sure, mate, no worries at all.”

Chapter 43

Our truck rolled out of Port Hedland. I gave the Esperanto hippie the thumbs up as we passed him so he'd know all was well, but he was back to spinning the basketball and ignored me.

Meanwhile, the driver's name was Robbo and he was an iron-mining explosives operator. He told me he spent sixty-five hours of his week in an underground, fifty-degree-Celsius hole in the earth.

"Sounds hot," I said.

"Naah, mate, naah," he said. "Try bloody summer underground—then it gets hot! Fifty-five! Talk about shit house!"

I did the math in my head: fifty-five was 131 degrees Fahrenheit.

"But Oi don't mind," he continued, swerving to avoid a roadkill kangaroo that had been hit the night before. "Oi work the mines so Oi can live in the bush. The pay's not at all bad, an' it supports me lifestyle quite well."

I looked out into the passing desert. It didn't look like there was anything out there—just miles and miles of empty, dry scrub.

"So you like living in the bush?" I asked, trying to sound upbeat.

“Mate,” replied Robbo, “the bush is bloody incredible! No ladies, Oi grant that, but Oi figure that’ll all change one of these years. This is still the frontier, after all.”

He went on to tell me about a pet camel he’d had a couple years earlier, and how she’d get jealous and spit at his friends when he brought them over to the house.

“Oi roped Fiona from me truck when she was just a little tackah! Shot ’er mum for meat—didn’t realize she ’ad a calf in tow. Kept ’er for neah four years ’til she up an’ run off into the bush with a mate of ’er own. There’s feral herds out there—roamin’ free as they loik. Brumbies an’ donkeys too. All got turned loose from captivity back before the turn o’ the century. They breed like bloody mad ’cause they got no natural predators. Nobody minds much if ya kill a few ’ere an’ there, ’cause all they really are’s a bloody nuisance to ’Stralia.”

As I nibbled muesli, Robbo went into a long side tale on the relative culinary attributes of donkey versus camel. He seemed to prefer donkey.

We passed the familiar turnoff to Marble Bar—now silent and empty. Its green roadsign flew by in a blur. I gave it a sad, silent look. Delilah’s face popped into my mind’s eye, then whisked away. I thought of sharing my experience from the night before with Robbo—but felt the timing was wrong.

"Yeah, mate, Oi got two hundred kilos of donkey stored back in the freezer at 'ome, an' Christ, Oi could probably add anothah thousand by tomorrow if Oi wanted. It's free bush tucker—not that feed-an'-'ormone shit ya buy in the grocery."

"Hmm," I replied, my stomach growling.

"Brumbie's not bad either, mate," he went on, "though Oi meself prefer donkey. Richer meat, more iron. Good for the blood an' the spirit. Keeps me young."

Chapter 44

More roadkill kangaroos dotted the road. I gazed out the window at their square, rotting muzzles and thick, whiplike tails. A thought popped into my mind—a desire.

"Robbo," I asked, "is it possible you could pull over the truck for a minute the next time we see a kangaroo skeleton so I can grab its skull? I've got a collection back home in America—and I have a sterile bag to put it in."

I tensed for a moment, unsure if he might not respond like my father—with disgust, the kind that risked causing him to rage at me later.

"No worries," he replied casually, slowing the truck to a reasonable speed, about thirty-five miles an hour.

"Thanks!" I said. "Awesome!"

Robbo, meanwhile, talked on.

"An' roo meat isn't bad either," he said, "jus' a little gamey. Rich in iron, though. The key's jus' not overcookin' it. Oi braise it meself—the loin—with peppers an' wild onion. Tendah!"

In no time at all we spotted a luckless roo—and pulled over to inspect. Unfortunately its skull was squished, the result of having been run over by a road train.

"Piss-poor," said Robbo, shaking his head. "An' smells like a rat gone bad."

Two more kangaroo carcasses, though, soon graced our path. Robbo identified the first, which I stored in my bag, as that of an adult male red kangaroo, which surprised me. For being a specimen of the largest roo in the world, it had a very small head—and an even tinier brain cavity.

But Robbo filled me in: "Christ, mate, kangaroos didn't get on Noah's goddamn Ark for their brilliance! 'Bout all they know how to do is hop, eat, fuck, an' fight."

Robbo turned over the second skull with the toe of his boot and identified it as a western gray. It was still in the process of decomposing and had little, foul clumps of grayish hair clinging to it.

But I didn't mind. I stored it with the other one and put their bag inside three plastic grocery bags, which I tied tightly shut. I didn't want the skulls stinking up my backpack or contaminating my food.

“Just be bloody careful with them at customs,” warned Robbo as I buried them under my clothes. “They’ll be nice skulls once ya clean ’em up, but they’re not worth jail time. Them baahstards at border protection don’t play games when it comes to conservation.”

“I’ll hide them in my dirty socks,” I replied.

Chapter 45

I stood alone in front of the desert roadhouse and watched Robbo drive away. Although I was two kangaroo skulls richer, I was officially stranded.

At over a hundred degrees, the land here had no naturally-growing trees, no plants of any decent size, no outdoor water—running, flowing, or even stagnating—and just miles and countless miles of the same yellowish-brown earth being baked into oblivion by the sun. Beads of sweat formed on my forehead and I drank a few sips of water to make up for the lost moisture. There was no town here, no bus stop, and not even room for a road train to pull in—only a wee roadhouse with a filthy toilet that didn't flush and a dry sink with a faucet that had been stripped of its handle. Using my fingers, I tried turning the square screw that activated the water but couldn't manage to create the leverage to get the thing to budge a millimeter. If I needed water here, I would have to buy it in the roadhouse. And it wasn't cheap.

The roadhouse lacked a prime location as well. Since it was a mere 140 kilometers from Port Hedland, most of the passing Broome-bound cars still had nearly full gas tanks and therefore lacked a decent reason to offer their patronage.

For the first hour of my wait not a single car pulled in. Lacking in options, I sat on the broiling shoulder of the highway to greet the oncoming traffic—oddly enough, the same traffic I would have greeted in Port Hedland had I just played it cool and stayed put.

I tried to hitch with all my energy, repeatedly falling to my knees on the pavement like some sort of desperate monk whenever northbound cars appeared, but in vain. Car after car stormed past going seventy or eighty miles an hour or faster, too fast to acknowledge my marginal existence. I caught mere glimpses of the faces of the drivers and their wives and their curious children staring out at me from their crowded back seat perches, wispy glimpses of the whites of their eyes.

In their lapses the road became silent. The sun became a glaring, heat lamp and sweat rolled from my hair in rivulets, quickly drying to a salty crust. A large, buzzing fly landed on my sleeve. I swatted him away and a moment later he landed on my head. I could feel him walking on my hair.

I journaled to distract myself. I wrote about my parents. I'd been pretty distant from them these past six months—calling home only sporadically, keeping it brief, hardly telling them anything. I was building a life here, a safe life of my own, and I needed to protect it with privacy. My mother had actually wanted to fly to Australia to visit me, but I had not liked the idea at all. She could be so needy—and so sad. I felt guilty about that, but I shuddered at the idea of her meeting my new friends. She had almost none of her own and throughout my childhood had claimed mine for herself.

Three more large flies landed on me. They were hairy and unafraid. They kept trying to crawl into my mouth. Swatting them away did nothing; they just landed again. They made it hard to concentrate.

I saw a dried-up roadkill kangaroo about fifty feet down the road, so I walked over to visit him. He was just a bit of fur, skin, and bones—and no moisture whatsoever. There were no flies on him—and he didn't even smell. Most of his vertebrae were exposed and I studied his morphology. He looked almost human—except for his tail bones and little, crushed skull.

I returned to my journal to write an addendum to my experience in the pickup truck the night before, but I couldn't concentrate. There were too many flies—twenty, maybe thirty now. They were extremely ticklish as they walked across my skin. They focused mostly on my face—my nostrils and mouth and ears and the corners of my eyes, wherever they could find liquid. Their soft, probing tongues were itchy and confident and made me twitch and flick my neck in response. I tried everything to get rid of them—screaming, flailing my arms, swatting, even burning toilet paper—but it all failed: in a moment they were back. There was nothing for me to do but sit and miserably accept them.

Chapter 46

Before too long, two northbound vehicles traveling in tandem pulled into the roadhouse. They were old folks and their cars were crammed full of chairs and tables and a whole load of other stuff—even a microwave. The husbands, the drivers, wore expensive, wrap-around-the-head ultraviolet sunglasses that molded into their soft, wrinkled flesh. The ladies, sitting in the passenger seats, wore elegant, flowery dresses. As they came to a halt along the petrol pumps, I burst from under my armor of flies and made chase.

At the driver's window of the lead car, I peeked my face down into his view.

"You headed north?"

I smiled and swatted an irrepressible fly off my nose. About five of my horde had already found me, and more were coming. I had to work fast.

"What's that ya say, son?"

He didn't notice the flies and rolled down the window to get a closer listen. My voice grew meek.

"Uh, are you headed north?"

The man blinked his eyes as he saw the intruders. Quickly rolling up his window to all but an inch, he shook his head.

“Sorry, mate,” he replied, poking his nose up near the crack, “we’re full-up.”

He then rolled up his window the rest of the way.

I tried the second car. Yet again my small winged friends followed me—but it was no use. The driver, whose vehicle was less full, had already made up his mind.

“Sorry, mate,” he stated before I even had a chance to ask, “the wife’s got asthma an’ we can’t handle us a passenger.”

I nodded my head in contemplation, realizing that taking me along would probably entail handling several passengers.

“Mmm, it’s cool.” I took a step back, a few flies buzzing around me. I didn’t swat them away. “No worries.”

Chapter 47

An hour-and-a-half later—during which time the flies ruined three more hitching attempts from the pumps—I watched two men in their mid-sixties in a nearly empty minivan roll up from the south and pull in. I sized them up as having excellent hitching potential and raced after them, this time with a new strategy: forthright honesty.

Wearing my kindest and most plaintive smile—and staying back about six respectful feet—I asked the driver for a lift. Then I explained my reasons.

"I've been swarmed by flies," I said, "and I can't seem to get rid of them. It's horrible. They're driving me crazy—and they scare everyone away. Please—even if you only drop me off at the next roadhouse, I will be forever indebted to you. By the way—you should probably roll up your window or they're gonna get in there on you!"

"Oh, I see!" replied the driver, pressing the automatic window button to seal his bubble. However, he seemed to be amused by me. "What a dis*aaaahs*ter!" he mouthed dramatically.

I nodded, smiled back, blew a fly off my lower lip, and mouthed my reply silently: "I know!"

I could see he was thinking about taking me along. He lowered his window about three millimeters.

"Well," he stated, "we're only goin' about two hundred kilometers more today."

"Anything is perfect," I replied. "Literally, *any*thing. You can even strap me to the top of the van!"

"Well, let's not go that faaah!" he said, laughing. Then he nodded slowly. "But ya should know—we have a dog: an' he sometimes bites."

That concerned me. I'd been bitten a few times as a kid—once pretty badly on the knee by a neighbor's doberman. Walking close to the van, I scoured its interior from top to bottom to see what I'd be getting myself into—yet saw no dog. Shuffling my feet, I put on a show of nonchalance.

But then I saw it: the canine.

It was a chihuahua. He emerged from underneath the seat, hopped up onto the driver's lap, and glowered at me through the window, shaking his lips and crooked teeth and snarling menacingly. He couldn't have weighed more than five pounds and looked about as threatening as an animated bath mat.

Judging the timing to be in my favor, I took the plunge.

"Can I risk the dog and hop in?"

He smiled.

"Yes," he said. "Yes—ya may. But we aren't licensed to carry passengers in the back. It'll be a squeeze, but ya'll have to sit up front with us."

Chapter 48

The single front seat of the cool, air-conditioned van was narrow, with plenty of space for two but barely enough for three. I sat between the driver, whose name was Reginald, and the passenger, who watched me curiously. The passenger held a full, open can of lemonade in his hand and said nothing. He too was a gentle-looking old fellow with a head of thinning, white hair. It suddenly struck me that they were a gay couple, but I wasn't sure.

"How's it goin'?" I asked the passenger.

He tilted his head to the side and offered no response. His eyes were thick and watery and unfocused and his lower jaw hung low with slack. His tongue fluttered nervously in his mouth. A stream of drool formed on his lower lip and rolled down his chin. He made no move to wipe it off and it dripped and collected in a soaking puddle on his lap.

I wondered if he had had a stroke.

Reginald fired up the engine and pulled out of the petrol station. As we rolled onto the highway, the chihuahua resumed its snarling at me. This seemed to click something in the passenger's mind and he opened and closed his droopy lower jaw a few times, swallowing.

"Tuh-tuh-Turk," he whispered, barely louder than the sound of the engine, "Turk, uh, um, nevah bit anyone."

The driver reacted. Leaning across me, he stuck his nose into the passenger's face.

"Furphy! Turk bit *Bah*bara. Twice." But that wasn't all. "An' Turk tried to bite Louise several times—remember that night on the boardwalk, Graeme?—an' also those two bogans on the catamaran." Then he turned to me, rolled his eyes up into his head, and lowered his voice to normal speaking tone. "That was the day we almost lost Turk to Sydney Hahbor."

As he steered us on forward, he used his free hand to scoop Turk up onto his lap and pat him lovingly on the head. Turk curled his lips at me and his thick tongue writhed in and out of his mouth.

I wanted to ask if they were a couple, but I didn't know how.

I'd never spent any time with a gay couple before.

And I didn't want to sound rude—or intrusive.

Chapter 49

The desert road swallowed us up and we were soon beyond the sights of civilization. Reginald cranked the air conditioner and I breathed a sigh of relief. Graeme sipped his lemonade but was so tottery that he soon dropped it. I had to snatch it up from his drool-covered lap before it spilled everywhere. Handing it back to him, I watched some liquid soak into the material of his golf shorts. Since both sides of his body seemed equally affected by whatever problem he had, I wondered if he had multiple sclerosis. Or AIDS?

I'd never met anyone with AIDS. And I had heard of cases in which one partner had it and the other didn't. But were they partners?

I wanted to ask, but it was Reginald who asked the questions instead. Yet he didn't ask them of me—rather, of Graeme.

"An' how *is* Louise doin'?" he asked all excitedly, his voice box bobbing up and down. "We haven't heard from her in quite some little time now, have we, Graeme?"

Graeme looked forward and said nothing, his face betraying no emotion. It was awkward.

"Well," replied Reginald, hopping in declaratively to save the moment, "of course ya must know that Louise was stung by that dreadful box jellyfish up in Queensland some months back—an' the nurse at the hospital where she was treated just happened to be related to Bahbara's ex-husband. Imagine that? All the way up in Cooktown! And then *Mah*garet, Louise's mother-in-law, who lives in Cairns, drove all the way up to visit her an' got her cah stuck in the mud an' had to be towed out! Ya know how much that cost her, Graeme?"

He seemed hopeful that Graeme would actually answer. Which he didn't.

"Two hundred an' seventy dollars!"

Chapter 50

Graeme drifted off to sleep. His head bounced off my shoulder with the shifts in the road and he drooled lemonade on my t-shirt. To make matters worse, when his face collided with my moist shoulder blade it jarred his thoughts and he would mumble out a string of incoherent words.

"Ba-ba-baba-ba-basically tryin' for na-na-na-nothing, mate."

Or: "Uh-uh-uh-uh-up in Sah-sah-sah-Sydney it's not ba-ba-ba-bad at–"

"–we stahted driving at six fifteen this mornin', Daniel," broke in Reginald, "because Turk woke us up. We had the alahm set for seven but the cheeky Turkster stahted baahkin' at five thirty!"

Using two fingers, he batted Turk on the head in mock anger. Turk curled up tightly in his lap and growled most enjoyably. Graeme fell silent.

I grunted to acknowledge Reginald, but he'd already darted off in a new direction, into a rather drawn-out story in which he and none other than Graeme had been on a road trip together in the wine country in South Australia many years before and had picked up another long-distance hitchhiker. Although the fellow, Reginald recalled, had looked somewhat like me, he'd had no gear at all, not even food or a toothbrush or a single cup of water—let alone a backpack.

"Imagine that?" he stated dramatically.

I sensed he was telling me the story for dual purposes—to forge some common ground with me, and also to let me know that he and Graeme had been together for a while.

Chapter 51

Reginald talked on and I listened. By piecing together bits of information, I learned that he and Graeme hailed from a suburb of Sydney and had been taking road trips all around Australia together in a variety of vehicles for decades. From this I concluded with greater authority that they were definitely, *probably* a gay couple—and that he probably wanted to acknowledge this to me, if only because he probably sensed that I was thinking about it and didn't know how to bring it up.

Choosing an indirect route, I devised a safe and seemingly innocent question that I hoped would broach the subject.

In a lull between tales, I asked, "Have you ever traveled to Tasmania?"

Tasmania, Australia's island state, is a place where homosexuality had been declared illegal. Being gay was an offense punishable by up to twenty-one years in prison. I had heard that it was called "Bigot's Island."

His happy reply, steering us along as pleasantly as ever and humming a tune to himself: "No, not yet."

Then to Graeme: "Maybe we could go an' visit Bahbara, Graeme. You'll have to ring her when we get back to Sydney."

Then to me: "Baaahbara is Graeme's cousin. She lives in Tassie—in Launceston. What a doll! Fifty-six an' looks not a fortnight past thirty-five!"

Then to Graeme: "Do you remember, Graeme, back when you had that dapper red coat?"

All I managed to piece together from this was that the two of them were definitely not related; Barbara, after all, was not Reginald's cousin.

Meanwhile, we had other important information to discuss. As always, there was the question of where we were going.

Reginald hit upon it first.

"Graeme an' I are staying in a little seaside cabin at a resort on Eighty Mile Beach. It's still a couple hours up the highway, Daniel, but if ya want to join us for the trip to Broome tomorrow ya're more than welcome to sleep in one of the extra beds. We'll have a lot of extras, of course now, won't we, Graeme?"

Graeme fluttered his eyelids on my shoulder, said nothing, and drifted back off to sleep.

Reginald then reminded me of my other option: being dropped off along the highway at whatever point I chose, presumably another dusty, fly-filled, hundred-degree, nearly carless roadhouse.

Put that way, my decision was simple.

"Sounds great. Count me in."

"Maaahvelous!" replied Reginald.

Chapter 52

The cabin was a small, musty box nailed into the dry earth. It lay tucked into a eucalyptus grove a few hundred feet off the beach. Its two rooms were set apart by an ancient, paper-thin wall, with only a doorless doorway cut into it to allow access to the inner room. The outer room doubled as the kitchen and dining room and had two small, single beds in its depths. The inner room contained a king-sized bed just beyond the doorway and two bunk beds crammed into the receding darkness.

"Choose a bed," commanded Reginald, "any bed ya want. Ya're the guest."

Thinking it over quickly, I chose one of the single beds in the outer room—giving them the better, more private room and a slew of options. I was curious which they'd pick.

As I sat on my bed Graeme marched past me and plopped himself down on the king-sized bed. Clearly it would be his. Reginald, carrying two armfuls of their things, was right on his heels and began piling their belongings onto it, definitively claiming it as their own. From this I concluded that they were a couple.

Reginald, meanwhile, took no further notice of me and devoted his attention to unpacking the van, carrying armloads of stuff—pillows, toiletries, food, clothing, a radio, slippers. He organized and reorganized the piles in a flurry and seemed full of nervous energy. His tension seemed to be coming from Graeme, who wasn't much of a help in the unpacking department. Graeme kept following Reginald back and forth and sitting down clumsily in the middle of each unpacking project, getting in the way.

"Stop it, Graeme!" Reginald cried out. "Can't ya see I'm tryin' to get some work done heah?"

Graeme, unfazed, tried to help out anyway and ultimately ended up dropping a box of their ceramic travel dishes onto the kitchen floor, breaking two. This caused Reginald to lose his cool.

"Now look what ya done, ya silly ding-dong!"

This crushed poor Graeme, who began weeping uncontrollably and stumbled blindly into the inner room, where he fell into a fetal position on the bed.

"Get up, Graeme!"

"Muh, muh, muh!"

Graeme shut his eyes.

"Stop that fuss now an' get up!"

"Muh, muh, muh!"

I sat on my bed, trying to pretend I wasn't witnessing the scene. I felt embarrassed.

Reginald turned to me in shame and stared at my boots.

His face grew serious and he looked me in the eyes.

"Uh, Daniel," he declared, "there's somethin' important I should tell ya. Would ya mind steppin' outsoid with me for a moment?"

My heart clenched in fear. I felt that this was the moment he was going to tell me that Graeme had AIDS. And I didn't know if I was ready to hear it.

Chapter 53

I forced myself to follow him out.

The late-afternoon sun was still in full tilt, a fresh breeze was rolling in from the Indian Ocean, and the eucalyptus trees around our cabin swayed to and fro, whistling and squeaking.

Reginald walked over to the van and began poking about inside it. I sensed he was nervous and pulling a diversion. After a few seconds he pulled his body out of the van, stood up to his full height, and turned to me.

"Daniel," he said, reaching out to take hold of my arm—then stopping himself before he touched me and retracting his arm, "what I have to tell ya is about Graeme."

His arm fell to his side. I blinked and tried to behave normally, though my heart was beating fast.

"Graeme," he said, staring me in the eyes, "is dyin' of Alzheimer's disease."

"Alzheimer's?"

"Yes," he replied, looking down limply. "That's what's the matter with him. It's the Alzheimer's. Early-onset. It's destroyin' his brain. He's had it six years—got diagnosed when he was fifty-eight. He's actually three years younger than I am. I, I—uh—thought ya should know."

"I'm sorry," I said, feeling myself drawn to him. I wanted to give him a hug, but stopped myself. I just wasn't ready. Instead I spoke. "My grandfather has Alzheimer's too. My dad's dad. It's not good. He's in a special home in California. My grandmother died a few years ago and no one wanted to take him in. That's why they put him there. He used to be a college professor."

The last time I'd seen Zaydee he hadn't recognized me. I had barely recognized him, for that matter. He had been strapped to a chair and had peed his pants. His whole crotch area was wet. I'd told the nurses, but it had taken them twenty minutes to come out and take him away to be changed. I had been the only visitor on his whole unit. The place seethed with loneliness.

Reginald smiled a wee bit, as if to acknowledge our commonality. Then he shook his head.

"I couldn't put Graeme in a home. I'd feel too responsible. I just couldn't do it. Back in Sydney they said I should—and I even visited a couple. They were awful and I wouldn't listen."

"He's lucky to have you," I said.

"Mmm," said Reginald. "Thank you."

Chapter 54

Later that afternoon the three of us took a hike along Eighty Mile Beach. It was low tide and the beach was an immense mud flat. I walked far out to the water's edge and took a swim in the shallow waves. I also gathered an assortment of Indian Ocean seashells for my collection, storing them in my pockets. A few looked familiar—cowries and olives and colorful mini-scallops. The rest were new.

Then, to give Reginald a break, I took Graeme for a longer walk by myself. As he trudged along by my side, I pretended he was my grandfather. We sat in the dunes and I tried to engage him in conversation, but without luck. After a long minute of silence, all he replied was, "Where's Reginald?"

I told him that Reginald had gone back to the cabin to get ready for dinner. I didn't ask him any more questions, though he seemed to like it when I sang him some old Yiddish lullabies—the ones Zaydee had taught me, brought over by his parents from Russia. From time to time Graeme hummed tunelessly along.

When we returned to the cabin Reginald donned an apron—"Grandma's Kitchen," it stated boldly—and rustled us up a hearty supper of bacon and eggs. It was my first meal in far too long that didn't solely include some permutation of muesli, apples, carrots, peanut butter, raisin cookies, and peach puffs. Mopping up the last of my egg with a slice of full-grain, garlic toast, I watched Reginald feed Graeme. He cut Graeme's food into neat rows and airplaned bites into his mouth.

"Vroom!" said Reginald. "Vroooom!"

The fork made its descent.

"Mmmm," muttered Graeme. "Mmm."

I watched with curiosity. I'd never seen a grown man feed another grown man, and despite its initial oddness I found it touching—and thought to myself that if either of them had been a woman I would have said they had a pretty conventional marriage, given the circumstances of the Alzheimer's.

At eight o'clock Reginald and Graeme settled into their king-sized bed together, under a large, single comforter. Both wore only underwear and had made no move to hide getting undressed in front of me. Eric's dad Arnold had done the same the night we'd shared a motel room in Southern Cross, but somehow that had felt different to me. I felt shy now.

“G’night, Daniel,” said Reginald, flicking off his bed lamp, “sleep tight.”

Graeme was already snoring loudly.

“G’night,” I replied quietly as I took out my contacts and rested my head on my pillow.

Chapter 55

I lay nestled in my sleeping bag on my box spring mattress. I stared up blindly at the ceiling and pictured the two of them lying on the other side of the wall—with an open doorway between us. I closed my eyes and tried falling asleep, which usually came easy to me, but I couldn't—even though I was physically exhausted and sunburnt.

I found myself thinking of my last week. I'd already hitchhiked more than three thousand miles—Melbourne to Perth, and now up the coast—and I'd hardly had a chance to process any of it. It was like a movie in fast-forward.

Just outside, the night birds and insects were singing a mad chorus of free song that filtered in through the dusty screen window. I tried meditating on the sounds, but couldn't concentrate.

My mind drifted to a conversation I'd had with father about my mother back in January, the night before I'd flown to Australia.

"She sometimes can't control her drinking," he had confided. "And I think it's getting worse."

"Did you talk with her about it?"

"She denies everything," he said.

"I know," I said. "It's always been the same for me. A few apologies the next day, and then she denies everything."

A charge of electricity ran through my body, igniting the thought that I wasn't looking forward to going home. I rolled to my other side and took a few slow, deep breaths to derail the train of thought. My pillow smelled like dust. I blew my nose into a tissue and put the dirty tissue into my backpack so Reginald wouldn't see it in the morning.

I then devised a mental exercise to relax myself: to think of where I'd spent each night on this journey.

My first night out of Melbourne had been in two parts. The first found me huddled awake inside my sleeping bag under a snowy pine tree outside a roadhouse in the Grampians, a mountainous national park en route to Adelaide. The second part found me sleeping in the passenger seat of an Adelaide-bound truck that had saved me from that hell. The truckie's name was Lefteris. He was Greek-Australian, and told me he'd come over from Athens in the early-70s to escape the dictatorship there.

The next night I'd slept in the passenger seat of a sheep shearer's car in the Nullarbor Plain of South Australia. The shearer's name was Angus and he had picked me up in Port Augusta—and had driven me over a thousand miles in his old Holden, due west. I'd been a little scared of him at first. He was rough, spoke quickly and in a half-incomprehensible shearer's dialect, and had big, muscular, hairy arms. And it didn't help that he'd shared that he had boxed semi-professionally a few years earlier. But eventually I realized how kind he actually was, and we had bonded. He was the first one on the road I'd told about my parents, and I had cried in front of him. He told me his parents had split up too. He said his dad used to beat up his mom, and finally she'd had enough and left. She was dead now, though.

Angus had also told gay jokes—"poofta" jokes, he called them. I felt guilty about that now, ashamed of how easily I had laughed. But they had made me feel comfortable then—him too, probably. So that was my second night.

My third night was with Arnold in Southern Cross. We had talked for hours—and I had cried in front of him as well. He had told me about his relationship with his wife—how they'd almost split up twice.

"Been married neah forty years, son," he'd said. "We've had our ups an' downs. Mostly ups, Oi must say, but some 'aahd times too —very 'aahd. Ya always 'ope it'll work out right 'n' proper, but sometoims life jus' 'as its own way with ya—that's what Oi reckon. Doesn't mean ya don't love each othah, but sometoims it gets too difficult. Not easy to be married in this crazy, modern world. An' Oi feel for your generation. It's only gettin' 'aaahder."

Then came the two nights on Eric's couch in Perth—a perfect break. It had also been nice to have friends my age—respectful friends. The sleep wasn't so great, though. The couch was lumpy and too short, and I'd had to sleep with my legs hanging over the edge. That was nights four and five.

Then I'd had the night in the truck with Caspar, night six, then the two with Nigel's family—seven and eight. I'd slept well there, but hadn't really felt comfortable opening up and being myself around them. They were good people, just too conventional—too proper—not on my wavelength. They didn't ask about my hitchhiking—only about my studies. And I never did tell them about my parents.

And last night, night number nine, I'd been in my tent in Port Hedland. The ground had been uneven and rough and I'd had a violent nightmare just before dawn. And it hadn't helped that there'd been a dog howling nearby the whole night long. I think someone had tied it to a tree or post. It sounded miserable. I had had to stuff moistened toilet paper in my ears to get some peace.

I took a sip of water and rolled back to my other side. I found myself imagining sharing my tent with Delilah. I pictured her reaching over and touching me. I shuddered.

Someone in the next room passed gas. I suspected it was Graeme.

Chapter 56

At half-past-midnight I lay in my bed, awake. The birds had quieted down but the insects were still going strong, humming away. My mind raced along as nimbly as ever. For the last hour I had been thinking about the kid with the Michael Jordan t-shirt. He had attacked me. I had been attacked while hitchhiking. If he had been stronger and those men hadn't come to my defense, I really could have been hurt. I might have had to fight. I hadn't been in a fight since I was thirteen.

It had actually been against a black kid—an African-American. He had given me a black eye and I'd given him a bloody nose.

"Drr," grumbled Graeme. "Drrrrr."

I realized it was pointless to try to fall asleep here. I had too much on my mind and couldn't let my guard down. I needed my own space. Silently digging my glasses out of my backpack, I put them on. Standing up barefoot on the floor, I stuffed my sleeping bag quietly under my arm and grabbed my travel clock.

I tiptoed across the kitchen and unlatched the front door carefully so I wouldn't wake them. Stepping outside, I closed it delicately behind me. The gravel was cold beneath my bare feet. The insects sang loudly all around me. I could see the outlines of the eucalyptus trees in the moonlight. I inhaled a deep breath. Trotting down the path toward the Indian Ocean, I left the cabin behind me.

Chapter 57

At six twenty my alarm went off. My body lay cozily snuggled in my sleeping bag in a hidden dune valley by the ocean. I had engineered a sand bed for myself, complete with a sand pillow. I rolled over to silence the beeping, then yawned. The sun, not quite risen, was bringing first light to the sky. Morning was on its way. I had slept for five good hours. I felt grateful.

I put on my glasses, which I'd hidden in my pocket inside some toilet paper so they wouldn't get lost or scratched. After brushing the sand off my things and out of my hair, I unzipped myself and climbed to the top of my dune. I looked to the ocean. It was a regal blue—almost purple. The tide was now high, submerging the mud flat. As I turned in the opposite direction, toward the inland horizon and the twisty rows of cabins, I saw the sunrise coming over the land. It was yellow and radiant—and warmed my face.

Today I would arrive in Broome.

Chapter 58

A few hours later the three of us were once again bouncing along northward, now through a land of dry, red earth and dead, yellow plants. I saw two wedge-tailed eagles soaring overhead, and a dead one on the side of the road next to a fresh kangaroo carcass. I didn't ask Reginald to stop, though not for fear that he was squeamish, but because I'd already found a dead wedge-tail outside of Brisbane a few months back and had plucked its tail feathers. They were bigger than a bald eagle's—and were waiting for me back in Melbourne, their quill tips doused in borax to keep away the bugs.

It was uncomfortable in the van. The air conditioner mysteriously refused to function and our bubble became a sauna—because Reginald was afraid to roll down the windows more than a crack for fear that Turk would make a leap for the road.

In a sad irony, of the four of us it was Turk, who, lacking sweat glands, took the heat the hardest. He snarled on and off for hours. Reginald told stories to pass the time and keep the peace. He was presently in the middle of one about a red kangaroo he and Graeme had hit en route to Ayers Rock some years back.

"It must have weighed over a hundred kilos," he said, eyes wide for effect. "It demolished the entire front end of our Volvo an' then went on to kick out the windscreen with its hind legs."

"Oh!" I replied.

I was curious, but really my head was elsewhere. We would soon be arriving in Broome—and parting ways. I would be going off on my own, probably to a hostel. It would be my first free and unhosted break since leaving Melbourne. I wanted to stay there a few days before returning to the road. I was planning on hitchhiking back east across the top of the country—to Darwin on the Timor Sea and then on to Queensland and the Great Barrier Reef.

"They had to call in the Royal Flying Doctor Service an' fly us to the hospital in Alice Springs to have the glass picked out of our faces. Graeme even had a chip in his eye. It was touch an' go for a while there."

In Broome I would try to make new friends—and I would buy food and cook. I would also clean my kangaroo skulls in the bathroom when no one was around. It was a dirty chore, but I didn't mind. They'd look so good when it was done. No one in America had kangaroo skulls.

“Quite a little bingle, that was. Isn’t that right, *Graeme*?”

No reply. Graeme had fallen asleep.

I would probably buy a pack of cigarettes too, and if I made some new friends who smoked I would share.

“Graeme was drivin’ then, Daniel,” said Reginald, sighing audibly. “That was before they took away his license, back when he was an urban planner—before his redundancy. We used to take turns behind the wheel. He could make me laugh like no one else. We used to go hours pretending we were bogans—full-on, accents an’ all. It was a routine we had. I was Mick an’ Graeme was Mack.”

“Hmm,” I laughed. “Mick and Mack. I like it.”

I would also call home—or then again, maybe I wouldn’t.

“I sometimes think,” said Reginald, “that I should write all this down—like a memoir. Truth really is stranger than fiction. An’ the ending is never what ya expect.”

And I would write. Write down all this. Write down my thoughts, my feelings, my fears, my hopes. Maybe I could write a memoir too—about this trip. The title “Up the West Coast of Australia” popped into my head—in bold blue letters on a yellow-brown and blue cover. The Outback sky across the desert land. I liked it. And I bet people would read it.

"You could call it 'Travels with Graeme,'" I said.

"I love it!" said Reginald. "'Travels with Graeme!' It'll be a bestseller! An' you'll be in it. A shinin' character on our trip up the west coast of 'Stralia: the tall, skinny, 'itchhikin' Yank, covered in bush flies, beggin' to join us like a lost child—an' now one of the family."

I laughed at the serendipity of his words: up the west coast of Australia. Yes, I had my title.

Oh, I would miss Reginald. And Graeme too. In their own special way they were my adopted granddads. They would have their own section in my book. And so would the Aborigines. And Caspar. And Murray. And Robbo.

"A breakaway bestseller," declared Reginald.

"Bah, bah, bah," said Graeme.

And I would study a map. Surely some traveler in Broome would have one.

Darwin, after all, was a long way off.

Epilogue

Nearly twenty-five years have passed since I hitchhiked from Perth to Broome. I am now more than twice the age I was then—and have lived a few lifetimes in the interim. Reginald, meanwhile, would be over ninety if he's still alive. And Graeme would be in his late-eighties, though it's hard to imagine he's still living. But you never know.

I didn't end up keeping in touch with them, but I have thought of them many times over the years—and I did offer the universe a private hurrah on their behalf four years later, in May of 1997, when I read the news that homosexuality had finally been decriminalized in Tasmania. I have often imagined that they took a road trip down there to celebrate.

I didn't actually keep in touch with anyone from that trip, though I did send Caspar a postcard of thanks from Niagara Falls a couple of weeks after I returned home—to the wreckage of my family. I put my return address on the card in case he wanted to write back, but he never did. And in a way that's okay. People on the road didn't exchange addresses much back then—much less last names. There was a freedom and spontaneity in the anonymity of it all, and in many ways I miss that freedom, that sense of really living in the present and for the present—of respecting what the present moment and the present interaction have to offer. That was, after all, the tail end of the era before the internet and smart phones and social media—and that sense of permanent, if at times a bit obligatory, friendship.

Meanwhile, to conclude my tale, I did end up hitchhiking to Darwin after Broome, and then over to Cairns and the Great Barrier Reef. I also hitchhiked a bit around northern Queensland, up through the mud and the rainforest, and had some more adventure, and a little romance too. Then I caught a bus back to Melbourne, and soon after a flight home.

A few months later, in early 1994, during my final semester in college, I began writing this book, typing it out on my old Mac Classic and saving the chapters to floppy discs. But I didn't finish it. Instead, once I graduated, I went traveling again—to Europe and Asia. The draft, which I called "My Australia Book," sat in my hard drive for a couple of years, percolating. I resumed writing it in 1996 in New York City, on a borrowed laptop in the Lincoln Center Library for the Performing Arts, and over the next year-and-a-half wrote a long draft—probably four or five times the length of this copy. It was a main focus of my life.

And then I tried to get it published: and couldn't. This was depressing, but in the long-run a good thing. I needed distance from it—and I needed to move on with my life. My parents had moved on with theirs—each having remarried new spouses in 1998.

And eventually I moved on too. In 1999 I went back to grad school and became a therapist—and built a ten-year career, which eventually led me into documentary filmmaking. Interestingly, my filmmaking brought me back to Australia a few years ago, and even to a screening at Melbourne University. My old friend Wombat, whom I'd kept in touch with for twenty years, showed up. He was married with three kids and lived in Wagga Wagga, in southern New South Wales. He taught primary school and wrote science fiction short stories in his spare time. He had gotten a couple published.

I had gotten a couple of mental health books published (and was about to self-publish a new one called "Breaking from Your Parents"), but Wombat didn't seem too interested in any of that. He was more curious about this book.

"So are ya gonna finally publish it?" he asked. "This is gettin' ridiculous. I'm gonna need bifocals to read it if ya hold off much longer."

"I hope," I said. "Someday!"

Back in the day I had read him some excerpts from my journal and he hadn't forgotten.

"'Specially that part where ya get beat up by that Aboriginal kid. Ya really need to share that. It's fuckin' literature, mate."

"Someday," I said. "Someday."

"An' ya also need to tell what happened with those kangaroo skulls. That's an important piece—'specially if ya ever want to come back into 'Stralia again."

"You're right," I said. "Good call."

And so, here it is:

Sadly, I never did bring home those two kangaroo skulls, though they did clean up quite nicely. I was just too scared—or too wise—to hide them in my luggage. I had a dream of returning someday to Marble Bar (which I still haven't done), and I had a weird premonition that those kangaroo skulls might just end up jeopardizing that future journey. So I adopted them out—to Wombat. And it is in his home in Wagga Wagga where they live, happily and legally, to this day.

The End

Acknowledgments

I wish to thank but a few of the people along the way who, by reading drafts of this manuscript and offering suggestions, have helped make this book a better one. They include Nick Garnock, Teresa Bergey, Joe Newton, Frederick Timm, and Alex MH. My gratitude to you. I also wish to acknowledge Peter Garrett, Robert Hirst, and Jim Moginie, the writers of the Midnight Oil song "Beds Are Burning," some of the lyrics of which I quoted.

Made in the USA
Las Vegas, NV
25 July 2023

75215891R00100